GAI PERRY

IMPRESSIONIST PALETTE

QUILT COLOR & DESIGN

C&T PUBLISHING

Copyright © 1997 Gai Perry

Developmental Editor: Barbara Konzak Kuhn

Technical Editor: Joyce Engels Lytle

Cover Design: John Cram and Kathy Lee

Book Design: Claudia Smelser Design

Illustrator: Kandy Petersen

Quilt photography by Sharon Risedorph; flower photography by Gai Perry;
author photograph by Jill Perry

Library of Congress Cataloging-in-Publication Data

Perry, Gai
Impressionist palette : quilt color & design / Gai Perry.
     p   cm
    Includes bibliographical references and index.
    ISBN 1-57120-030-4 (pbk)
     1. Patchwork—Design. 2. Quilts—Design. 3. Fabric pictures.
4. Landscape in art. 5. Impressionism (Art) I. Title.
TT835.P449124 1997
746.46'041—dc21   97-6598
                                                          CIP

Chaco-Liner is a registered trademark of General Pencil Company.
Fairfield Low-Loft and Fairfield Soft Touch are registered trademarks of Fairfield Processing Corporation.
Mountain Mist and Quilt Light are registered trademarks of Stearns Technical Textiles Company.
Omnigrid is a registered trademark of Omnigrid Inc.
Setacolor is a registered trademark of Pebeo France.

Published by C&T Publishing, Inc.
P.O. Box 1456
Lafayette, California 94549

Printed in Hong Kong

10 9 8 7 6 5 4 3 2

TABLE OF CONTENTS

Dedication 5

Foreword 7

Introduction 8

ONE Impressionism in Art 11

Impressionism in Quilts 13

Landscape Vocabulary 14

TWO Color Imagery 16

Color Theory 17

The Spectrum 21

The Influence of Color 25

Color Enrichment 30

Harmonious Color Schemes 32

Contrast 38

Color and Design Questionnaire 39

THREE The Fabrics 43

What Kind and How Much? 43

Floral Prints 44

Examples of Flower Scale
and Square Size 46

Element Prints and Textures 53

FOUR Cutting Methods 59

Making a Design Board 62

The Design Process 64

Additional Design Techniques 67

FIVE General Project Instructions 71

Land, Sea, and Sky 72

The Incredible Flowering Tree 78

Monet's Garden 86

Field and Stream 92

Victorian Bouquet 98

Les Fleurs 104

SIX Sewing the Landscape 109

Borders 115

Quilting 116

SEVEN Thoughts on Creativity 118

Questions and Answers 120

Template Patterns 124

Bibliography 126

About the Author 127

Index 128

Vase with White Roses, 1996, 22" x 23¼", Gai Perry

DEDICATION

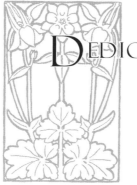

Flowers speak a language of love, friendship, and caring. They help soften the edges of sorrow, and their natural beauty increases our enjoyment of grand scale celebrations and quiet moments. Who can resist the allure of a romantic floral painting, or a bouquet of daisies clutched tenderly in the hands of a child? Flowers give so much pleasure it's no wonder gardening has become a favorite recreational hobby. Well, I like to garden in theory…but not necessarily in practice. Every year, just as the first iris are starting to bloom, I get a heady case of "spring fever." I smile and daydream a lot, and wiggle my toes in the warming earth. Somehow I find the energy to weed a couple of flower beds before making my annual pilgrimage to the nursery. As I walk among islands of "earthy delights," the fragrance and colors become so intoxicating that my self-control completely vanishes and I gather a staggering assortment of blooming annuals. I buy them in pots, in flats, and even in seed packets. My intention to plant is always sincere, but somewhere along the way I get an idea for a new landscape quilt and forsake the garden for my studio. The flowers sit on my deck and eventually wither and die. I know; it's sad! But the truth is, I'd rather be "gardening with fabric!"

So to quilters everywhere, who would like to plant gardens in their sewing rooms, this book is dedicated to you!

Serenity Bay, 1995, 57" x 60", Gai Perry

 FOREWORD

Life is full of surprises! Circumstance, opportunity, happy accidents? What determines the paths we take? My husband and I met and married in New York City. The day after our wedding, we put all our worldly goods into the trunk of a rental car and drove to California. It was a profound decision, made on the spur of the moment. When we said good-bye to family and friends, I wasn't the least bit sad. I was so young...all I could think about was moving to a place where I'd be able to swim in the ocean every day.

A year and a half later we were living in a tiny apartment in San Francisco next to a very cold Pacific Ocean. We had a colicky new baby who would be awake from three in the morning until noon. What to do with the time? I tried baking bread, but watching dough rise gets old quickly so I bought some watercolors and taught myself how to paint. It turned out to be my salvation! As the years went by, whenever I had the opportunity, I painted for recreation, remuneration, and mental health. The style I settled into was called photographic realism, and I worked with oils and then later on, acrylics.

When we became more affluent, we bought a house in the country and I started collecting antiques. Eventually, I opened an antique shop and learned how to restore and refinish furniture. I considered it another form of artwork. Then, in 1981, I discovered quilting. The fabrics! The colors! The patterns! The quilt block is a wondrous thing: abstract art in its purest form. I spent several happy years making, then later teaching classes in traditional quilt design; but, in 1990, I got an urge to start painting again. As a grand finale to what I considered was my quilting career, I thought it might be fun to try something a little more contemporary, something that hadn't been done before. Since I'd always been attracted to the work of the French Impressionists, I came up with the idea of translating impressionism into a quilt style. The Impressionists' paintings are so full of color and vitality, and I like the intentional vagueness of their quick, bold brush strokes...it leaves something for the imagination to play with.

Although I explored various methods of landscape design, including appliqué and strip-piecing, nothing seemed to mesh with either my feelings about impressionism or my comfort level. Eventually I originated a style of quilting that uses hundreds of small squares, set on-point, to illustrate a scene. I named it "The Art of the Impressionist Landscape." The technique becomes more complex as I grow older, but seven years later the bloom is still on the rose. It seems as though my professional life has come full circle. I'm painting again, but this time, with fabric.

INTRODUCTION

A beautifully designed quilt combines the dimensional texture of a sculpture with the graphic coloration of a painting. Take it off the bed, hang it on the wall, and it becomes Art!

Someone said that Ginger Rogers could do everything Fred Astaire could do—but she did it backwards and in high heels. Hooray for us! It's taken three hundred years, but women are finally getting some credit for their accomplishments. Looking back, it's hard to imagine there was a time when quilting was one of the few ways a woman could express her artistic vision without appearing lazy or frivolous. We've come a long way....and the patchwork quilt has traveled right along with us.

In the seventeen hundreds, while pioneer women were making scrappy One-Patch and Log Cabin quilts, their city sisters in Boston and Baltimore were fashioning elegant *Broderie Perse* and Album quilts. Later, during the Victorian era, crazy quilts were in vogue and as Americans moved through the first half of the twentieth century, patterns like Grandmother's Flower Garden and Sunbonnet Sue became popular. Today there is an explosion of contemporary quiltmaking. Quilters seem to be pushing the boundaries in every direction trying to "reinvent the wheel." Sometimes the results are breathtaking; other times a bit over the edge, but what's important to note is that like our ancestors, we're once again exploring new territory.

One of the new territories we're exploring is the pictorial landscape quilt. As we become more adept at translating our design ideas into fabric, we're unlocking doors that discriminate between making pictures with cloth (quilts) and painting on canvas. These days, quilt artists are devising ingenious ways to interpret nature and there are some exceptional books available. Joen Wolfrom's *Landscapes and Illusions* presents her graphic strip-piecing method, while Katie Pasquini Masopust takes a more abstract approach with *Fractured Landscape Quilts*. There are also two other lovely landscape books written by Ruth B. McDowell and Charlotte Warr Andersen. In 1995, I joined this literary group of quilt artists when I wrote *Impressionist Quilts*. After my work was published, I was sure I'd experience some kind of closure on this design style...but it didn't happen. I continued buying floral prints, and so many ideas for new projects kept whirling around in my head that before I knew it, I'd made ten more quilt tops. It seemed a second book was in progress; but, if I was really going to write it, what could I include that would make it a better, more complete volume than the first? As my mind wandered through the possibilities, it kept stopping at color. Lustrous color harmonies and artfully blended floral prints are what inspire a viewer to make an Impressionist Landscape quilt. Since working with color has always been one of my favorite passions and pastimes (and the reason I started making quilts in the first place), I decided I'd write about it.

There is no doubt that some people have an inherent sense of color and can put together a pleasing group of fabrics with little or no effort. But for others the process is difficult. They feel insecure with their selections and rely on friends and quilt teachers for help. If you fall into this category, please read the Color Imagery section (starting on page 16) to learn a definitive method for selecting fabrics and designing color schemes. You'll find out what a subjective palette is, and you can fill out a questionnaire that reveals your willingness to experiment with color. You'll be challenged to "see" color, and then to organize it in ways that make it a reflection of your individuality. Working with color should be a pleasure, not an ordeal. I hope you'll enjoy reading the section as much as I enjoyed writing it.

There are six new landscape projects in this book, and once again they're arranged in sequential order from easy to not-so-easy. Those of you who have worked with my first book will find some contradictions in method and some new techniques, so it would be a good idea to read everything leading up to the first project. It will make your design experience more pleasant. Besides, reading is good for you. It exercises the eye muscles, and heaven knows we need all the exercise we can get!

❦

Making one of the Impressionist Landscapes is an artistic adventure, and the sewing is easy—just some simple piecing of different size squares on-point. All your energy can be channeled into selecting beautiful flower fabrics and arranging them in a composition that from a distance looks like a lovely painting. This is as close as you can get to being a painter without actually knowing how to paint. There is only one problem. Like eating potato chips, you can't make just one quilt. As soon as you show it to a friend, she's going to want one just like it. Or your husband will insist on hanging it in his office. So be forewarned. "Gardening with fabric" can become addictive, although I can't think of a more delightful or relaxing habit.

Poppy Fields, 1995, 30" x 27", Gai Perry

Poppy Fields,
1995, acrylic on canvas,
Gai Perry

IMPRESSIONISM IN ART

Impressionism is a painting style that looks at nature through rose-colored glasses...a romantic blend of light and shadow, softened outlines, and brilliant colors. At its heart is the passionate exploration of transient (changing) light and its effect on color. Whether the Impressionist was painting a backyard garden scene or a country meadow, the color harmonies remain so lustrous, so pure, one really does get a feeling of sunlight shining from the canvas.

The word impressionism was coined in 1874 by Louis Leroy, a French art critic, as a negative reaction to a Monet painting entitled *Impression, Sunrise*. The label stuck, and a group of artists including Renoir, Sisley, Manet, and Monet began calling themselves Impressionists. They painted *en plen aire* (outdoors "in open air"), away from the controlled atmosphere of the studio. Their style was to work quickly, using little dabs of several pure colors to illustrate each element in the composition. There are no flat, one-color surfaces in an impressionist painting, nor are there many clearly defined edges. The artists used a series of gradual color and value changes to move from one area to another. This subtle blending contributes to the reflective quality of the paintings.

As word of this flamboyant new painting style spread beyond the borders of France, artists from all over the world came to Monet's home town of Giverny to study and absorb the natural beauty of the area. One of the artists who traveled to Giverny was a young American named Guy Rose. I discovered his work when I attended a 1995 retrospective at the Oakland Museum of California. His paintings overwhelmed me, and as I walked from one sunlit canvas to the next, I felt a compelling desire to own one. Not possible, of course, but during the following week I spent several hours thinking about his work. I was attracted to his paintings because his color choices were so similar to mine; if not in my quilts, at least in my head (we'll talk more about this later). I was particularly drawn to a field of brilliant red poppies and decided to do something I hadn't done for years. I dusted off my paints and brushes and tried to create an impressionist painting. Although I'd never worked in the impressionist style before, after a few hours of experimentation my picture was finished and I was surprisingly pleased with the way it looked. It wasn't a Guy Rose by any stretch of the imagination, but it was mine and I could hang it on the wall to enjoy. Then I took the process a step further and made a quilt from my painting. Both the painting and the quilt are shown at left.

My Garden Room

When I walk into this room, I immediately feel more at peace, more serene. I love the mixture of quilts, paintings, and white wicker furniture. This is a place where I can daydream, read a book, or share tea and conversation with a friend. There is a wall of glass facing my garden and even though my flowers need more tender loving care than I have the time to give them, I'm frequently rewarded with a spectacular view of blooming rose bushes and hardy perennials that flourish in spite of my neglect.

IMPRESSIONISM IN QUILTS

An Overview of the Technique

Translating impressionism into a quilt style was a labor of love and not nearly as difficult as one might expect. The Impressionists' method of color blending, which was to use several colors to interpret each element in a painting, is perfectly suited to tone-on-tone and textured fabrics. When several of these fabrics are cut into small squares and then sewn together, they blend visually, giving a dramatic layering of color. These subtle combinations are perfect for elements like water, trees, hills, and sky. Solid color fabrics, although tempting because of their wide range of hues, are inappropriate because they project an image that is too flat and non-reflective.

Value-graded and color-graded prints are used to transition from one area to another. This method creates the soft, blurry edges that are so typical of Impressionists' paintings. Many fabrics are used on both the front and the reverse side to help achieve this gradual movement of color and value.

Floral prints with dark backgrounds are more effective than those with light backgrounds. This is simply because the colors are more intense. Also, florals with light and dark background can't successfully be put in the same quilt. If they are, wherever a light background square appears, it looks like a hole in the quilt. Floral prints with black, navy, and dark green backgrounds are interchangeable. When the correct size flowers are chosen, most of the dark backgrounds will disappear after the quilt is sewn.

A 1¾" finished square seems to be just the right size to encompass a single flower. By doubling and tripling the finished measurement, larger flowers can be incorporated into the design. Rectangles are also used occasionally and all the shapes, no matter what their size, are placed on-point rather than in straight rows. The on-point position allows the fabric squares to blend in a more artistic fashion and helps to create the illusion of an impressionist painting.

You will be designing your quilts on a vertical surface and all the squares will be in place before the first stitch is taken. This method allows you the opportunity to improve and make changes in your landscape as it develops. Many of the floral print squares are cut individually, using templates to insure that one whole flower fits within the seam allowances. This is necessary because it's the image of the intact flowers that makes the finished quilt look like a real picture, not just a wash of colors. The individual cutting may sound tedious but once you get into the spirit of it, you're going to have fun searching for just the right kinds of flowers to plant in your garden.

LANDSCAPE VOCABULARY

These terms will be used throughout the book. If some of the definitions seem unclear, don't be concerned. After reading the Color Imagery section (starting on page 16), and then actually beginning the hands-on design process, the vocabulary will start making more sense.

Base square   The base square in an Impressionist Landscape always measures 1¾" after it is sewn. This finished measurement may be doubled, tripled, or even turned into a rectangle to accommodate larger scale flowers. A complete set of template patterns starts on page 124.

On-point   All squares are set on-point (set at a 45° angle to the sides of the quilt) and sewn into diagonal rows. A triangle will need to be placed at the beginning and end of each row to render the quilt "in square."

Natural elements   An Impressionist Landscape is composed of natural elements. Flowers, water, trees, sky, foliage, hills, mountains—anything pertaining to nature is considered a natural element.

Value-contrasting areas   A pleasing contrast of values will make an Impressionist Landscape more interesting. For this reason it is desirable to establish areas that can be interpreted with light, medium, and dark value prints. Elements like sky, water, and grass are usually the lightest value areas. Flowers, as a whole, read as the medium value areas, and foliage, hills, and mountains are most often the darkest value areas.

Color-contrasting areas   The contrast between the warm-colored flower areas and the cool-colored sky, hills, and foliage.

Palette   This word is used to describe a compatible group of colors. A quilt executed in a personal palette should reflect a composition of one's favorite or "signature" colors.

Color family   I've reduced the twelve-color circle to six color families: red, orange, yellow, green, blue, and violet. Each family has its own group of tints, tones, and shades. For example, the color blue ranges from blue-violet to blue-green. (See page 30 for a detailed explanation.)

Color-related prints   A selection of fabrics from one of the six color families.

Tone-on-tone print   A print that has two or more shades and values of the same color.

Value-graded print   A print that illustrates a value movement from light to dark.

Color-dominant print   A print that has a main color but is also enriched by subtle touches of other colors.

Fabric personality   This term helps to define and categorize the nature of a print: floral, texture, stripe, plaid, etc.

Transition   To transition means to move from one element area to another, using prints that are value and color graded. When this is done gracefully, the movement is gradual and softly impressionistic.

Soft-edge   Refers to the fuzzy impressionistic lines that define each area and element in a landscape. Soft-edges are created by using the transition method described above.

Hard-edge   Just the opposite of a soft-edge. A hard-edge is defined by a distinct change in value and/or color.

Focus   The focus is what first captures the viewer's attention. It could be a path, a gate, some light frothy water, or even a stone wall. The focus can be a recognizable object or a dramatic contrast of value and color.

Print scale   Refers to the size of the repeated image on a fabric.

Distance   To establish a foreground, middle ground, and background in your design, make the elements in the foreground look larger and brighter. Gradually, as the eye moves toward the horizon, elements will become smaller, lighter, and less clearly defined.

COLOR IMAGERY

Imagine waking up one morning to discover that the world had lost its color. Your home and everything in it had faded to shades of black and white. Now imagine what your life would be like if this condition were permanent; the sense of loss you'd experience at never being able to see the colors of Christmas, or the intense blue of a summer sky. Many of us take color for granted. It surrounds us but we don't really "see" it, and when we dream, even though our subconscious mind spins a Technicolor extravaganza, all we can usually remember is a shadowy *film noire*.

Twenty years ago I was painting landscapes and portraits, but I wasn't really "seeing" the colors. That awareness came later when I started making quilts. Implausible as it may sound, the physical act of working with fabrics—touching and arranging them in color and value groups—has helped me to understand how colors interact; how they compliment or even insult each other. I've learned that the arrangement of colors, like the choreography of a dance, should have a graceful rhythm; a controlled pattern that leads the viewer's eye around the surface of a quilt. Color is the first thing you notice when you look at a quilt. Is the color combination powerful, elegant, playful? If the colors strike an emotional chord or are so beautifully arranged that you feel compelled to take a closer look, the quiltmaker has succeeded in his or her attempt to catch your attention. To keep your attention, and gain your admiration, the piece must be constructed with precision and quilted with small, even stitches.

To make an Impressionist Landscape quilt that combines the aesthetics of a good painting with the textural quality of an expertly sewn quilt, you need to fulfill a few basic requirements.

1 **Knowledge of the medium:** Research the subject. Find a good basic how-to quilt book (see page 126 for suggestions). Apply color theory principles when you are selecting a color scheme, and learn how to combine fabrics in a way that is both personally pleasing and artistic.

2 **Technical skill:** Acquire the ability to measure, cut, and sew accurately.

3 **Proper tools:** Always work with a sharp rotary blade and scissors, and have a smooth functioning sewing machine. Don't be frustrated by inadequate tools. They slow you down and break your concentration.

4 **Intuition:** This is your sixth sense. It tells you when your color and design choices are working. Learn to trust it! Creativity is an intuitive process. A phrase that con-

stantly runs through my head when I'm designing a quilt is: When in doubt, don't. If I feel insecure about any part of the design, I won't start sewing until the problem is solved. If I can't solve it to my satisfaction, I put it away. Maybe at a later date I'll have the knowledge to figure it out.

❧❧❧

In my first book, *Impressionist Quilts,* I outlined some rules that relate directly to a twelve-color circle. I said these rules are generally successful because they're based on natural laws governing harmony and contrast. Now let's go a step further and consider the use of subjective color (a personal set of colors that defines us as individuals). When we look through a book of contemporary quilts we can frequently identify a particular quiltmaker by his or her consistent use of the same color combinations and fabric personalities. Color choices can be as identifying as a written signature and by the time we're grown, we've developed a fondness for some colors and an aversion to others. Because color choices are such a candid reflection of our personalities, it's helpful to understand why we choose the colors we do. The Color and Design Questionnaire, at the end of this section, will help you find whether you've developed a palette and style that reflects your personal taste (not a composite of friends', teachers', and quilt shop salespersons'). While I was writing this questionnaire, I uncovered some surprises about my own work. My favorite color is turquoise, but for some reason I'd never made a turquoise quilt. Even though the Guy Rose painting exhibition helped me to recognize my first choice of color combinations, until I filled out the questionnaire, I'd never consciously made a quilt focusing on those colors. Perhaps when you fill out the questionnaire, you'll discover some surprises, too.

As you read through this section, you'll find the emphasis is on encouraging you to use a greater variety of fabrics in your quilts, and to develop confidence in your ability to make intuitive color choices. The information isn't limited to the Impressionist Landscape technique. It can also be applied to traditional and contemporary quiltmaking.

COLOR THEORY

I'm sure that, by now, you're familiar with the twelve-color circle and its related collection of terms and definitions. But, if not (and for those of you who need a refresher course), the following pages define a simple color vocabulary.

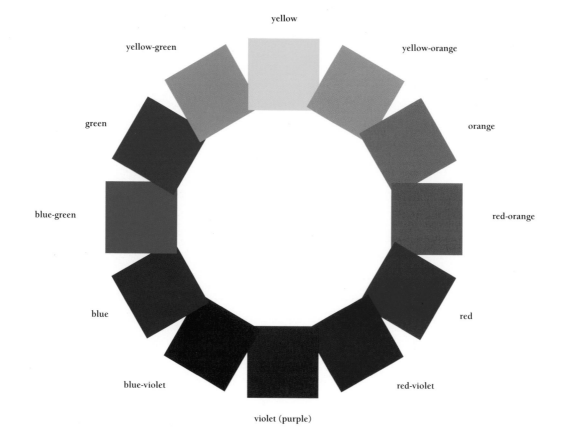

The Twelve-Color Circle

Primary colors   Red, yellow, and blue. These are the only three colors that can't be created by mixing other colors together.

Secondary colors   Orange, green, and violet. These colors are made by mixing equal parts of two primary colors.

Tertiary colors   Yellow-orange, red-orange, red-violet, blue-violet, blue-green, and yellow-green. Tertiary colors are created by mixing equal parts of a primary color with a secondary color.

Hue   Synonym for the word color. Chroma is another synonym.

Pure colors   All the colors on the color circle are pure colors. Pure in the sense that they haven't been altered with the addition of white or black to dilute or darken.

Saturation   The intensity of a color. Pure colors are fully saturated. When black or white is added to a color, it becomes less saturated.

Value   The degree of value of a color relates to the amount of black or white that has been added. The addition of black not only dulls the intensity, it also darkens the value of a color. The addition of white dilutes the intensity and makes the value of a color lighter. The value of color isn't always easy to judge because value can be relative. A particular shade of blue could be the medium value in one quilt and the dark value in another quilt. It depends upon the colors used near it.

A Value Scale in Blue

Cool colors   Tints, tones, and shades of blue, green, and violet are considered cool colors. They visually recede and are effective when used as backgrounds. When designing a quilt, it takes two or three times as much of a cool color to balance the impact of a warm color.

Cool Colors

Warm colors   Tints, tones, and shades of red, orange, and yellow are considered warm colors. They give the illusion of occupying more space. They also move optically toward the foreground. Warm colors have more intensity than cool colors.

Warm Colors

Complementary colors   Pairs of colors that are opposite each other on the color circle: red and green, orange and blue, yellow and violet, yellow-orange and blue-violet, red-orange and blue-green.

Tint   A mixture of a pure color with white. The more white that is added, the lighter the resulting pastel color will be.

Tints

Shade   A mixture of a pure color with black. The more black that is added, the darker and duller the color will be.

Shades

Tone   A mixture of a pure color with white and black (gray). The resulting color is mellower than a shade and not as delicate as a tint.

Tones

Black and white   Technically, black and white are not considered colors but we use them frequently to establish a more emphatic degree of contrast.

Detail of *Full Spectrum Garden*; 1995, whole quilt 33½" x 25", Gai Perry

THE SPECTRUM

The spectrum is a series of colored bands diffracted and arranged in order of their respective wavelengths by the passage of white light through a prism. To understand this definition, try to visualize a giant rainbow as it spreads its glowing bands of colored light across the sky. The simultaneous appearance of sun and rain create the illusion of light through a prism and we have a spectrum in all its natural glory.

The spectrum colors will always appear in the same order, and since the dawn of time when man first began to look at rainbows, certain powers, myths, and magic have been attributed to each of the spectrum colors.

Red

Red sits at the top of the rainbow and it's the most powerful color in the spectrum. Red is the color of blood and can generate passionate feelings of love, anger, aggression, appetite, and patriotism. People who favor red tend to lean toward physical pursuits rather than intellectual introspection. They have outgoing personalities.

A true red has neither orange nor violet overtones. Fabric dyes are successfully able to produce a pure red color but when a red quilt is photographed and reproduced in a book or a magazine, it will often appear red-orange. Printers use a different primary color system (cyan, magenta, and yellow); perhaps this has something to do with it.

Red is an attention grabber! I know this is true from personal experience. One day last spring, I was driving along the highway when I saw the mostly intensely pure red poppies I'd ever seen. I was so busy looking at them I almost drove off the road. The conclusion here is obvious: If you want your quilt to be noticed, put some red in it.

Green

Green is a combination of blue and yellow and it's visible enough to be considered the fourth primary color. Green represents life and rebirth. Along with blue, it's the dominant color in our environment. If you favor green you are presumed to be level-headed, consistent in your ways, and socially minded.

Green is the perfect background color. Envision a garden in full bloom. Immediately your mind's eye will notice the bright flowers, but what helps make the flowers appear so vivid is the contrast of the lustrous green foliage. Green makes warm colors look better. Green is a popular choice for quilters, and because we are familiar with the hundreds of tints, tones, and shades of green in our environment, we feel comfortable using it in our quilts. Green is our "security blanket" color.

Orange

Orange combines the light-giving qualities of yellow with the bold power of red. This blending results in a warm, friendly color; somewhat less aggressive and intense than its two parent hues. People who are attracted to orange are thought of as easy going and pleasant tempered.

The color orange is synonymous with the fall season. It's seen in the warm glow of a harvest moon and in the flaming tones of drying leaves. It is the color of bonfires, ripe persimmons, and fat pumpkins. Flowers like zinnias, marigolds, and tiger lilies will be the focus of any garden. Orange is especially attractive with its blue complement, but it works equally well with blue-green (turquoise) and blue-violet. Touches of orange in an otherwise cool-colored landscape will add a lively energy.

Blue

Blue is cool, soothing, and serene. We humans have a love affair with blue, and it calls to us like no other color in the spectrum. If blue is your first choice, you want to live in a peaceful world and you like your surroundings organized and tidy.

Blue is as infinite as the sky in its ability to change character. It can range from a gentle gray-blue to a vibrant cobalt. Along with green, blue is a favorite color for quilters. But, unlike green, even when blue is used as a background color, it maintains its primary importance and seems to dominate the color scheme.

Pure blue flowers are rarely found in a garden. I couldn't find any blue flowers to photograph, so I used silk hydrangeas instead. Flowers that we think of as blue, like delphiniums and bachelor buttons, are really closer to blue-violet and purple. When I buy a floral print that has some pure blue flowers in it, I always try to include them in a landscape; but, sadly, they never seem to blend with the other, more naturally colored flowers. My students go through this same intuitive process and pure blue flowers are often discarded from their landscapes. Happily, there are more than enough floral prints with toned-down blues and blue-violets to satisfy our cravings.

Yellow

Yellow is the color of sunshine and I think that perhaps there are more yellow flowers than all other colors put together. Yellow symbolizes intellect and enlightenment. It's a color for the "creative spirit." Those of you who put yellow in your quilts are considered to be strong-minded and self-assured.

Yellow is the most brilliant color in the spectrum and, when it's paired with its purple complement, forms a dazzling contrast of light and shadow. Tones of yellow and gold set against lavender and purple were particular favorites of the French Impressionists.

Because yellow is so intense, a little goes a long way. Just as a few rays of sunlight filtering through a window can lighten and energize a room, a touch of yellow in your landscape can make all the other colors appear to sparkle.

Violet

What is the color violet? We aren't even sure whether it should be called violet or purple. We know that it is a combination of red and blue, and our perception of the color can range from delicate spring lilacs to the hard-edge color used in Amish quilts and contemporary artwork.

Throughout history, violet and purple have enjoyed a religious, mystical connotation. It was thought to be an aristocratic hue; certainly not a popular working class color like blue. People who like violet are said to have the soul of an artist or a philosopher and prefer to "rise above the crowd."

Violet, mauve, and lavender were frequently used by the French Impressionists. I associate the color with fragrant flowers like heliotrope, hyacinth, and heather. Aside from using lots of violet-colored flowers in my landscapes, I also use the color to suggest distant hills and twilight skies.

Woodland Tulips,
1995, 25" x 20",
Gai Perry

THE INFLUENCE OF COLOR

When you think about it, the influence of color on our lives is astonishing. Hardly an hour goes by when we don't make some kind of decision based on our acceptance or rejection of a color. "I like the green dress better than the blue one; These tomatoes look nice and ripe; The sky is turning gray, I think it's going to rain." Whether we're stating a color preference, making a judgment call about the ripeness of fruit, or offering an educated guess on what the weather will be, we're using our ability to process color information to form an opinion. Color can also influence our mood and sense of well-being. When we surround ourselves with colors we're comfortable with, we feel more attractive, more at ease. I could never live in a room that was painted orange (even a pastel). It gives me shivers just thinking about it. But walls that are painted a soft grayed turquoise... that's my idea of heaven.

One of the nice things about human nature is that we're all different. I don't know if it's a good thing or a bad thing, but no two people interpret color in exactly the same way. My concept of a pure red might be entirely different from yours, and both of us are right because color perception is in the eye of the beholder. I teach color classes and one of our exercises is to spend a few moments preparing a list of colors we associate with each of the four seasons. When we compare the lists, the differences are fascinating. Some lists include ten colors for each season, others only three or four. And the palettes are entirely different. These are the colors I associate with each season:

April Showers, May Flowers, 1995, 33½" x 31½", Gai Perry

THE COLORS OF SPRING

All through spring, the hills where I live are covered with blankets of lavender and yellow wildflowers. Tiny shoots of grass are a delicate yellow-green. Everything looks fresh and new. I see spring colors as tints...lots of white added to soften the impact.

Fourth of July and Berry Pie, 1995, 30½" x 34", Gai Perry

THE COLORS OF SUMMER

In summer, I love the color of early evening sunlight. The air is hot and breathless and the landscape appears to shimmer under a halo of brilliant gold. Summer colors are vibrant. Pure saturated colors dominate the landscape.

Fall Collage, 1995, 31" x 36", Gai Perry

THE COLORS OF FALL

Fall vibrates with elegant russets and amber. The atmosphere is crisp and clear. Fall is a time of change. Crops are harvested, leaves are turning. The intense colors of summer are beginning to mellow. Gray is added, turning pure colors into toned colors.

California Winterscape, 1995, 33½" x 31½", Gai Perry

THE COLORS OF WINTER

In winter, the earth is sleeping...colors are shaded with black. It is a season of sharp contrasts. The landscape is covered with snow and branches of trees are etched against a cold, gray sky. Forests of ancient pines are mirrored in icy streams. Everything is darkness and light.

The Flower Bed, 1996, 25½" x 23", Gai Perry

COLOR ENRICHMENT

Color enrichment is a concept I've taught for several years in my traditional quilting classes. The phrase describes what occurs when several fabrics with related hues are combined to interpret the essence of a single color. Most fabric prints, even those rendered in a monochromatic color scheme, aren't limited to just one shade of a color. For example, an orange floral will incorporate several tones of yellow-orange through red-orange. The subtle addition of these hues enriches the personality of the fabric without altering the monochromatic color scheme. The Impressionists used this same technique in their paintings. Little dabs of red-violet, violet, blue-violet, and blue would visually blend to create an iris border or a field of wild lavender.

To gain a better understanding of color enrichment, let's put aside the twelve-color circle and concentrate on the six spectrum colors. For each color, we'll create a color family that incorporates a range of closely related hues.

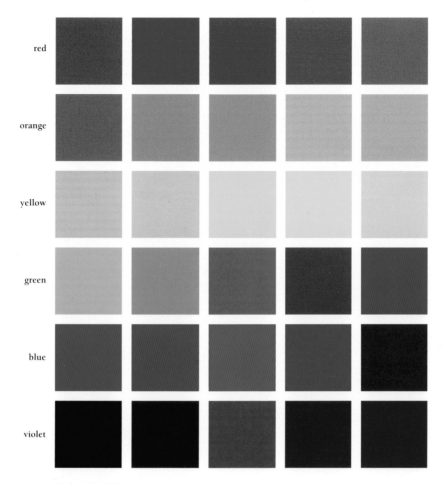

red

orange

yellow

green

blue

violet

Color Families

This is how color enrichment works. Let's presume that you want to make a traditional pink and green scrap quilt like the one shown on the following page. To begin with, instead of choosing several prints that have similar shades of pink and green, choose from a color family of pink and green prints that range from red-orange through red-violet and from blue-green through yellow-green. Then branch out and add some pink and green prints that have subtle amounts of other colors in them. The whole essence of color enrichment is to add as many colors as possible without changing the integrity of the original color scheme. Why do this? The answer will become obvious when you see the results. Your quilts will have an enhanced palette and they will be infinitely more attractive. The pink and green *Flower Bed* quilt, on page 30, shows how color enrichment can be applied to the Impressionist Landscape technique.

I've been using this method of fabric selection ever since I began making quilts. At first it was intuitive, then later when I started teaching, I analyzed my approach to color blending and gave it a name. All of the following color schemes can be improved by using the color enrichment technique.

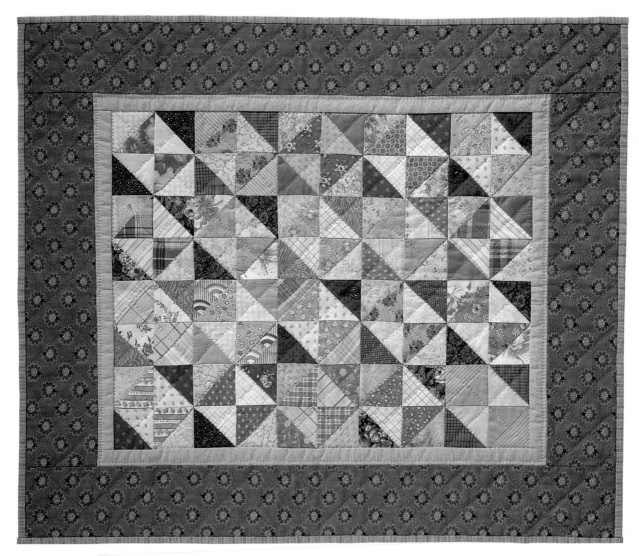

Broken Dishes, 1984, 25" x 22", Gai Perry

HARMONIOUS COLOR SCHEMES

When you are working with color you must accept the fact that nothing is absolute. There isn't a color rule that can't be bent or broken to fulfill your concept of a design. A color scheme should function as a starting point, a vehicle to help you select a compatible assortment of fabrics. Keep in mind that you are in control. At any point you can break away and skew or enrich the arrangement of colors. The five color schemes, shown on the following pages, are generally accepted by color theorists to be attractive organizations of color. I've illustrated each of them with a vignette (a small quilt that functions like a rough sketch). The vignettes were executed quickly and their sole purpose is to define a color scheme. I've chosen gold, which is in the yellow color family, to act as the focus color in each of the examples. Because black and white are technically not considered colors, they can be included in any color scheme without disrupting the composition of hues.

Monochromatic Color Scheme

This color scheme uses several tints, tones, and shades of one color in varying degrees of value. Because only one color family is involved, a quilt rendered in a monochromatic color scheme will indicate a definite mood and temperature depending on the warmth or coolness of the chosen color. It's a good choice for water scenes, but it would be difficult to design an impressionistic garden scene using this color scheme because contrasting green leaves are evident in most floral prints. However, you could still project the "feeling" of a monochromatic garden by using several kinds of flowers from either the red, orange, yellow, purple, or blue color families. Cut the squares of fabric so that the emphasis is on the flowers, not the leaves. What's left of the leaves will function as a subliminal contrast. The vignette explores a brownish-gold color in a value range from white to black. There are also small touches of green in the flowering branches hanging over the water.

Neutral Color Scheme

My impression of neutral is that almost any color can be considered neutral if it's so diluted with white or gray that it becomes non-controversial. A neutral color scheme can easily turn into a very ordinary looking quilt; but, with a little thought, you can "enrich" grays, tans, and beiges and make a quilt that is quite elegant. Be sure to include lots of white and some slightly darker neutral tones for contrast. Also include some neutral hues that lean toward pink and peach. This will give the quilt a nice "blush." My vignette uses a pale version of gold in the sky, along with some light peach at the horizon line. The water and the beach are rendered in a wash of soft colors that leaves it to your imagination to guess where the water ends and the sand begins.

The closest I've come to making a neutral quilt is *California Winterscape* shown on page 29.

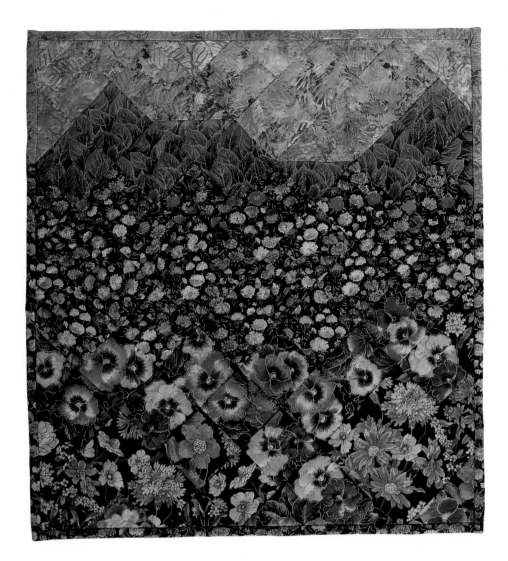

Complementary Color Scheme

Each of the twelve colors has a complementary color that sits directly opposite it on the color circle. A pair of complementary colors does just what the name implies, it enhances the best attributes of each. When complementary colors are placed next to each other, they become more intense. A superb example of complementary contrast can be found in one of the many self-portraits by Vincent Van Gogh. In the portrait I'm referring to, he painted his clothing and the background in shades of blue and turquoise, then he painted his beard a fiery orange. The contrast is powerful!

A complementary color scheme is satisfying because there will always be a built-in contrast of warm-cool colors. In the vignette, gold is combined with yellow and yellow-orange. The complementary color is an enriched blend of violet, blue-violet, and red-violet.

Analogous Color Scheme

An analogous color scheme combines three or four colors that are adjacent to each other on the color circle. It's the most reliable of the color schemes because of the close association of the hues. An analogous color scheme is perfect for waterfalls and woodsy landscapes. Personally, I find it difficult to design a landscape in this color scheme because I miss the contrast of the warm-cool colors. For the example, I had to use adjoining yellow, green, and blue color families to feel comfortable. When I work with an analogous combination like purple, blue, and green, I can't resist jarring it with a few touches of crimson, red-orange, or yellow.

Hydrangeas, 1995, 26½" x 28½", Gai Perry

Polychromatic Color Scheme

All colors, anything goes. Most Impressionist Landscapes will be worked in this color scheme. Choose two or three dominant colors and then add several subordinate colors for accent. This time my focus color is minimal, but because yellow is the most brilliant color in the spectrum, the flowers stand out.

CONTRAST

A real estate agent will tell you that the three most important things to consider when buying a house are: location, location, location! In quiltmaking they are: contrast, contrast, contrast.

Contrast is the pairing of opposites to create an enhanced product. Think about the contrast of a warm, berry cobbler with frosty vanilla ice cream or a black velvet dress with pearls. The contrasting elements make the individual components more desirable. Contrast should be considered when you're designing a quilt, and this is particularly true of an Impressionist Landscape quilt. Without contrast, a landscape can look bland and lack definition. The following types of contrast are important to the successful completion of landscape design. You should try to incorporate as many of them as possible.

1 **Contrast of value:** Even the simplest composition is improved by including some light, medium, and dark value fabrics. Generally speaking, in a landscape design, the flower areas will read as the medium value, the hills and foliage as the darkest value, and the grass, water, and sky as the lightest value. Before beginning a landscape, take a moment to define the value areas and choose fabrics accordingly.

2 **Contrast of warm-cool colors:** In most landscapes it's the contrast of the brightly colored flowers set against a background of green leaves, foliage, and blue sky that gives the viewer an impression of intense color. By using the color enrichment technique (described on pages 30–31) to select fabrics for the cool-colored areas, you can make them as visually interesting as the warm-colored flower areas.

3 **Contrast of saturation:** The charm of this contrast will become apparent as you become more adept at designing landscapes. If you can successfully mix saturated colors with duller shades and tones, the landscape will look richer and certainly more artistic. The trick is to work gradually from duller colors to brighter colors. If you were to put a darkly shaded flower in the middle of a group of bright flowers, it would look out of place. It would be better to move gradually from bright flowers, to toned flowers, to shaded flowers. Designing a landscape this way will also give the viewer a nice feeling of sunlight and shadow.

4 **Contrast of fabric scale and personality:** A traditional quilt with an overabundance of small-scale floral prints isn't nearly as much fun to look at as one which also includes some plaids, stripes, and geometrics. This is also true of an Impressionist Landscape quilt. Use a variety of flower sizes (just as you would if you were planting a real garden). Also, the addition of other elements like hills, trees, and sky make the flowers look more appealing by contrast.

As I stated earlier, most design and color rules can be effectively bent or broken. An untrained folk artist breaks them intuitively, producing a work of art that has charm and originality. A trained artist will knowingly break them, and turn something that is technically good into something that is artistically great. When I insist that an Impressionist Landscape must have contrast of value, prove me wrong! Make one with consistently intense medium-value colors and make it sizzle. In quiltmaking, as in any creative endeavor, you should be willing to take risks. It probably won't cost more than a few yards of fabric and some extra time, but the feeling you'll get when you turn out the best quilt you've ever made is worth the effort.

COLOR AND DESIGN QUESTIONNAIRE

There are no right or wrong answers, but you'll need to have read the preceding Color Imagery section to be able to understand all the questions. After reviewing your answers, you should have a clearer understanding of your color and design preferences, and whether you're using them effectively in your quilts.

1 Name your three favorite colors in order of preference.

1 _____

2 _____

3 _____

2 Do you use these favorite colors in your quilts?

☐ Yes   ☐ No   (Check one box.)

3 What is your favorite color combination? Name two to four colors.

1 _____

2 _____

3 _____

4 _____

4 Do you use pure, intense colors in your quilts?

☐ Always   ☐ Sometimes   ☐ Rarely   ☐ Never   (Check one box.)

5 Do you use pastel colors in your quilts?

☐ Always   ☐ Sometimes   ☐ Rarely   ☐ Never   (Check one box.)

6 Do you use dark colors in your quilts?

☐ Always   ☐ Sometimes   ☐ Rarely   ☐ Never   (Check one box.)

7 Do you use neutral colors in your quilts?

☐ Always   ☐ Sometimes   ☐ Rarely   ☐ Never   (Check one box.)

8 Do you use black in your quilts?

☐ Always   ☐ Sometimes   ☐ Rarely   ☐ Never   (Check one box.)

9 What type of colors do you use most frequently?

☐ Bright colors   ☐ Dark colors   ☐ Pastel colors   ☐ Neutral colors
(Check one box.)

10 Do you prefer to make quilts with:

☐ Very little contrast   ☐ Lots of contrast   ☐ Don't know   (Check one box.)

11 Do you prefer:

☐ Warm colors   ☐ Cool colors   ☐ Like them equally   (Check one box.)

12 Do you try to combine warm and cool colors in your quilts?

☐ Always   ☐ Sometimes   ☐ Rarely   ☐ Never   (Check one box.)

13 Which type of color scheme is your favorite?

☐ Monochromatic   ☐ Neutral   ☐ Complementary   ☐ Analogous
☐ Polychromatic   (Check one box.)

14 When selecting fabrics for a quilt, do you try to combine small-, medium-, and large-scale prints?

☐ Always   ☐ Sometimes   ☐ Rarely   ☐ Don't think about it   (Check one box.)

15 When selecting fabric for a traditional quilt, do you try to combine prints with a variety of personalities (stripes, plaids, florals, checks, etc.)?

☐ Always   ☐ Sometimes   ☐ Rarely   ☐ Don't think about it   (Check one box.)

16 Name any colors that you are reluctant to use.

1 _____

2 _____

3 _____

4 _____

5 _____

If you listed any colors, do you think they're associated with unpleasant memories? Sometimes knowing the answer to this question will help you overcome your reluctance to use a particular color, or at least allow you to understand why you don't like it.

17 Do you prefer:

☐ Contemporary quilts ☐ Traditional quilts ☐ Both (Check one box.)

18 Do you prefer:

☐ Designing your own quilts ☐ Working from a pattern ☐ Both (Check one box.)

19 Do you know how to draft a quilt block?

☐ Yes ☐ No (Check one box.)

20 Are you satisfied with your color and design skills?

☐ Yes ☐ Do you think there's room for improvement? (Check one box.)

❧❧❧

Now that you have defined your color and design preferences, take the information and consciously apply it to the first landscape project. If your personal palette has a narrow range of colors and you're comfortable with it, use several tints, tones, and shades of those few colors to provide additional character. If you like cool colors, make a quilt that looks serene; or, if you prefer complementary color schemes, design a landscape that is enriched with a variety of colors and fabrics. Whatever your preference, make the next quilt an obvious statement of your personality.

The Window Box, 1996, 33½" x 36", Gai Perry

THE FABRICS

Quilters are natural born collectors. We take pleasure in acquiring and storing "things." When I was young, I had a passion for storybook dolls and trading cards. Over the ensuing years I've collected antique furniture, china, folk art, Oriental rugs, quilts, and paintings. Now I collect fabric! Great quantities of it. Sometimes I think buying fabric is the best part of quiltmaking. When I walk through the door of my favorite quilt shop I'm like a kid in a candy store. Hundreds of succulent fabrics line the walls, and the anticipation of what I'm going to buy is always a delicious treat. I usually take at least an hour gathering an assortment of goodies, and while I'm in the store I talk with friends, discuss works in progress, and dish the current gossip. The whole experience is thoroughly satisfying. I suspect most of you feel the same way I do about collecting fabric so I'm sure the time you spend putting together a group of florals and textured prints for an Impressionist Landscape will hardly be a chore.

The night before I taught my first Impressionist Landscape workshop, I lay awake wondering if I'd be able to teach the technique effectively, and whether my students would go home feeling satisfied with the experience. As it turned out, worrying was a waste of time. A person's landscape quilt is as good as his or her collection of fabrics, and no amount of inspired teaching or hands-on help can compensate for a limited supply. So let's start collecting!

WHAT KIND AND HOW MUCH?

As you start building your collection, it would be better to buy smaller amounts of more fabrics. Instead of choosing two yards of one fabric, buy half-yard pieces of four fabrics. Although 100% cottons are preferable, a blend is acceptable if the print is too enticing to pass up. Just remember to press the blends with a cooler iron to prevent shriveling. The heavier weave decorator cottons are also compatible, and combining different weight fabrics doesn't seem to effect the appearance of the finished quilt. Pre-washing is optional. I skip this step because I don't want to lose any fade protection that might be built into the manufacturer's sizing. However, I will test a fabric for colorfastness before using it.

Get into the habit of looking at both sides of a fabric. Many times the reverse side has a softer, more subtle presence that can be effective when you're trying to transition from one color or value area to another. There's no law that says only the front of a fabric can be used, and I make this comment only because I'm surprised to discover how many quilters are reluctant to use the reverse sides.

You will be looking for multicolored florals and for prints with textures that give the impression of water, hills, sky, trees, grass, and foliage. Solid color fabrics are inappropriate because they lack the subtle texture needed to reflect light. On the following pages you will find examples for each fabric category, and I indicate whether the squares need to be cut individually (using a template) or strip-cut into squares with a rotary cutter. Complete cutting instructions begin on page 59.

FLORAL PRINTS

Flowers are the main focus of an Impressionist Landscape and the more color and variety of flowers you can squeeze in, the better your landscape will be. As you shop for floral prints, it would be advisable to concentrate on flowers that have the correct print-scale rather than choosing them because you like the color. I know this will be difficult now that you've identified your favorite colors, but try to keep an open mind and shop as though you were planning an extravagant mixed bouquet. Later, as your collection grows, you can design some of the specialized color schemes you've read about in the Color Imagery section.

Look at the floral requirements for the first project and gather those before spending a fortune on flowers that may not work. By the time you're finished with

Detail of a "wonder fabric"

the first project, you'll have a clearer idea of what to look for. I'm uncomfortable giving a specific number of floral prints needed for each project because it depends on the versatility of the fabrics you've chosen. There are a few floral prints (I call them "wonder fabrics") that have such a lovely variety of flowers and colors, it's possible to design a whole quilt using just one of them. Wonder fabrics are easily identified because they look like a garden in full bloom. They have small-, medium-, and large-scale flowers—giving you the option of using more than one size template. When I come across one of these versatile fabrics, I buy several yards.

All floral prints under consideration should include leaves. This is important! You will notice that each of the swatch examples have some kind of leaf in the print. Floral prints without leaves will look unnatural in a finished landscape.

❧❧❧

The floral prints you select for a landscape should be compatible in three ways.

1 Flowers that are viewed from the same distance should have a similar print scale.

2 Flowers need to have the same kind of personality. Some floral prints look very realistic. Others appear to look more painterly, as if they'd been rendered with an artist's brush. Still others are stylized to suggest a geographic location (flowers with an Oriental flavor) or a historical time period (flowers designed to look like crewel embroidery). Try not to mix the personalities.

3 Floral prints look better when they are arranged in tinted, toned, or shaded groups. Varying degrees of intensity may be used in different areas, but the movement from one area to another should be gradual. You can create sunlight and shadow effects by using tinted colors for the light areas, and toned and shaded flowers for the darker areas.

Note that all the fabric swatches on the following pages are shown slightly smaller than actual size.

Individual Flowers for 2¼" Squares and Corresponding Triangles

Flowers in this category should always be cut individually, with a template, to ensure that one flower fills the entire area within the ¼" seam allowance. Select floral prints with dark backgrounds only. Refer to page 13 for a detailed explanation. When you study the examples, you will notice that all the flowers are cut so they appear to be growing toward the top point of the square.

Individual Flowers for 2¼" Squares and Corresponding Triangles

Flowers for 4" Squares and Corresponding Triangles *(opposite)*

After they are sewn, one 4" square is equal to four 2¼" squares. Use the same criteria given for the 2¼" flower squares; however, now you have the opportunity to focus on more than one flower. This larger size is always cut individually with a template.

Flowers for 4" Squares and Corresponding Triangles

Flowers that Grow in Masses for 2¼" Squares

Many low growing flowers such as pansies and alyssum cluster together. Select prints with dark backgrounds only. These floral prints can usually be strip-cut into 2¼" squares with a rotary cutter.

Flowers that Grow in Masses for 2¼" Squares

Flower-Leaf Transition Prints for 2¼" Squares

A transition print is a relatively small-scale flower and leaf combination. Its function is to help ease the movement from one element area to another. The leaves blend into the grass and foliage, while the flowers blend into the larger scale floral areas. Sometimes transition prints can be strip-cut with a rotary cutter, but depending on how they are printed on the fabric, they may have to be cut individually with a template so they will look like they're growing skyward. Choose medium-dark and dark background prints only.

Flower-Leaf Transition Prints for 2¼"Squares

Mid-Distance Meadow Flowers for 2¼" Squares

Look for small-scale floral prints that have leaves and at least three or four flowers framed within the square. If you're designing a meadow and have placed larger flowers in the foreground, the mid-distance and far-distance flowers should have a similar color scheme. Use medium-dark and dark backgrounds only. Squares in this category can be strip-cut with a rotary cutter.

Mid-Distance Meadow Flowers for 2¼" Squares

Far-Distance Meadow Flowers for 2¼" Squares

These floral prints are an even smaller scale than the mid-distance flowers. Sometimes just the right printed texture can be used in place of a flower. For an example refer to *The Incredible Flowering Tree* quilt on page 78. Use medium and dark backgrounds only. Frequently, only the reverse side of the fabric is used in this category. These prints can also be strip-cut with a rotary cutter.

Far-Distance Meadow Flowers for 2¼" Squares

Combining Different Size Squares, Rectangles, and Triangles

All the larger size squares and rectangles are based on multiples of the 2¼" base square, which measures 1¾" after sewing. This page illustrates how some of the different sizes fit together.

Combining Different Size Squares, Rectangles, and Triangles

Inappropriate Floral Prints

The examples are all attractive floral prints, but when they are sewn into a landscape they look like pieces of fabric stuck in an otherwise realistic picture.

FLOWER SCALE
IS TOO LARGE

BACKGROUND
INTERFERES
WITH FLOWERS

LIGHT BACKGROUND

FLOWER SCALE
IS TOO SMALL

TOO MUCH
BACKGROUND
SHOWING

FLOWER PRINT
IS TOO DARK

FLOWER PRINT IS
TOO STYLIZED

FLOWER PRINT
HAS NO LEAVES

Reflections, 1995, 56½" x 50½", Gai Perry

Detail of *Reflections*

ELEMENT PRINTS AND TEXTURES

If you were to look outside on a sunny day (city dwellers will have to use their imaginations), you would notice that cool colors are dominant. The sky is blue, and the grass and trees are various tints, tones, and shades of green. But, as quilt artists, you can use your artistic license to exaggerate, change, or enhance…just the way Mother Nature does when she colors a landscape. You can make sunsets streaked with apricot and gold, or you can design violet mornings and foggy-gray afternoons. Foliage can range from pale yellow-green to a green that is almost inky black…or it doesn't have to be green at all. It can be a blend of turquoise, purple, and cobalt. You can control the colors of your landscape in any way you choose; all you need are the right fabrics.

Prints with nature themes are becoming more available every year. Textile designers have awakened to the contemporary quilt artist's need for an expanded variety of textures that reflect elements in the environment. For the last couple of years I've been collecting element prints and I was able to design *Reflections* without feeling the need to use a single flower.

On the next few pages you'll find examples of every type of element print necessary to design an Impressionist Landscape. Element prints should be cut into 2¼" squares only. If you try to save time by cutting them into larger squares, they will look obvious and "blocky" in the finished landscape.

Grass Prints for 2¼" Squares

I like to use light- and medium-value prints for grassy areas. Select tone-on-tone prints and textures that project a feeling of grass. You may even come across a fabric that's specifically designed to look like grass. Squares for grass can be strip-cut with a rotary cutter.

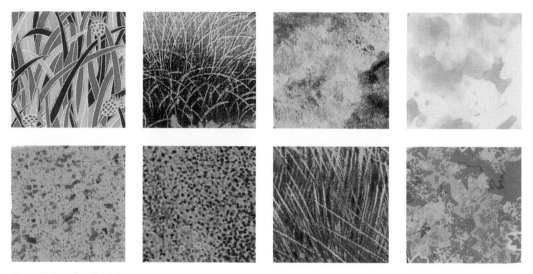

Grass Prints for 2¼" Squares

Leaf Prints for 2¼" Squares

When a landscape pattern suggests using leaves, it's usually referring to fabrics that look realistic and are printed with leaf shapes. They can be found in light, medium, or dark values. Squares for leaves can be strip-cut with a rotary cutter.

Leaf Prints for 2¼" Squares

Foliage Prints for 2¼" Squares

Foliage prints can be vague because they are usually placed toward the background of a landscape to give the feeling of distant trees and bushes. Look for tone-on-tone and color-dominant prints. Medium- and dark-value prints are preferred. Foliage squares can be strip-cut with a rotary cutter.

Foliage Prints for 2¼" Squares

Water Prints for 2¼" Squares

Choose tie-dyes, batiks, and textures that look liquid. You can use value-graded fabrics like the examples shown on the two lower rows, or blend several different fabrics that look compatible. Squares for water can be strip-cut with a rotary cutter.

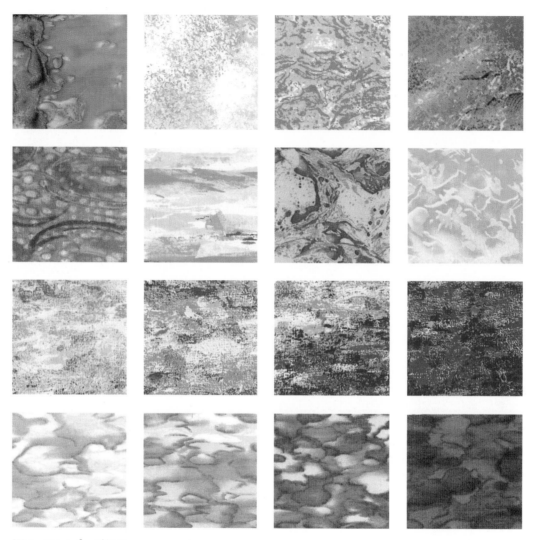

Water Prints for 2¼" Squares

Sky Prints for 2¼" Squares

I rarely use more than one fabric for a sky because I think it looks lighter and more airy if it's kept simple. Use your imagination to create a lovely multi-hued sky with batiks or marbleized fabrics. If your landscape looks too busy, try a soft cerulean blue sky texture for a calming effect. Sky squares can be strip-cut with a rotary cutter.

Sky Prints for 2¼" Squares

Hill and Mountain Prints for 2¼" Squares

Hills and mountains can be just about any color you want, but I would suggest that you choose darker value prints of the same colors that appear in the sky. The combination will give a nice impressionistic blending of the two elements. The swatches show how to value-grade fabrics from the darkest print on the left to the lightest print on the right. It's a good idea to choose sky and hill fabrics at the same time, so you can develop a smooth movement of value and color. The squares can be strip-cut with a rotary cutter.

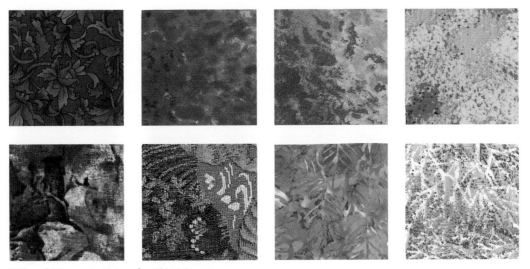

Hill and Mountain Prints for 2¼"" Squares

Path Prints for 2¼" Squares

Path prints are usually the lightest value element in a landscape. Look for light-colored floral prints that, when used on the reverse side, give the feeling of a sunlit walkway. Tan or gray gravel and rock-type prints are hard to use in this situation because the neutral shades are difficult to blend with the more colorful flower areas. Squares for a path can be strip-cut with a rotary cutter.

REVERSE SIDES

FRONT SIDES

Path Prints for 2¼" Squares

Object Prints

Object prints contain rocks, bricks, fences, houses, critters…anything that can be used as a focal point in your landscape. Use your discretion as to the size needed to be cut. You might have to use a larger square or a rectangle to make the object fit.

Object Prints

CUTTING METHODS

After collecting your beautiful new landscape fabrics, what do you do with them? Why cut them up, of course...but not all at once, and not until you start a project. My technique requires that you cut squares from a fabric only as you need them. When you begin working on a landscape, there will be step-by-step instructions concerning what to cut. For now, I'm just going to explain how to cut. You will need the following tools:

Sharp pair of fabric-cutting scissors

Rotary cutter and mat

"See-through" template plastic

Scissors to cut the template plastic

White Chaco-Liner® for marking dark fabrics and a fine-point black permanent pen for marking light fabrics

Ruler marked with quarter-inch increments (Omnigrid® or a similar style ruler) for accurate cutting and measuring

Begin by making a complete set of templates. The template patterns start on page 124. Trace the outside edge and the ¼" seam allowances onto template plastic using the fine-point black pen (no dull pencils, please). Cut out the templates with paper-cutting scissors or a blade.

INSTRUCTIONS FOR HAND CUTTING 2¼" FLOWER SQUARES USING A TEMPLATE

Move the 2¼" square template around a floral print until you find a single flower that fills up the area within the seam allowance. Because all the squares will be set on-point, it is necessary to position the flower so it looks like it's growing toward a point. Mark the fabric with a Chaco-Liner or black pen and cut the square with fabric scissors (or carefully cut around the template with a rotary cutter). Use whichever method feels more comfortable. Follow the same procedure when you are working with larger squares and rectangles. You will find that, because of the positioning, many of the squares will be cut off-grain. Don't be concerned until you start cutting triangles. Then, whenever possible, cut each triangle so that the longest side is on a straight grain.

Helpful Hint: Some of my students take the template patterns to a plastic fabricating store and have permanent templates cut from clear ¼" thick plastic. This makes rotary cutting easier.

RIGHT   WRONG

Cutting Individual Flowers On-Point

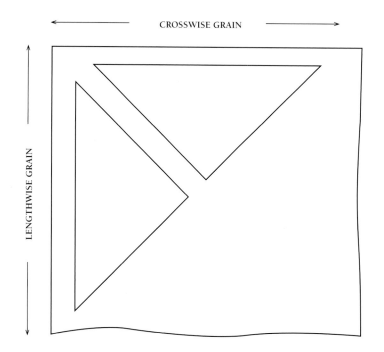

Cutting Triangles on the Grain Lines

Most element print fabrics may be cut on the straight of the grain using a rotary cutter. With your ruler, measure and cut a $2\frac{1}{4}$" strip, then cut the strip into $2\frac{1}{4}$" squares. Occasionally, you may have to cut a strip on a 45° angle to accommodate the direction of a printed texture. Rule of thumb: The direction of the print (for example, streaks in a sky fabric) should run parallel to the horizon.

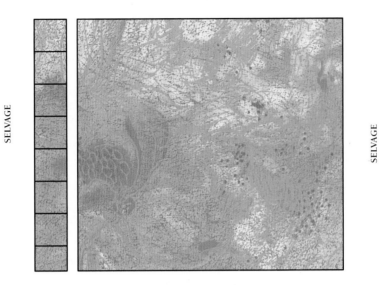

Cutting Strips on the Straight Grain

Cutting Strips on a 45° Angle

MAKING A DESIGN BOARD

Because you are going to design a quilt that will eventually hang on a wall, it makes sense to design it on a vertical surface (just as though you were a painter working at an easel). To make a design board, you will need:

One piece of white 100% cotton flannel (at least 36" x 45")

#2 lead pencil that will make a clean, dark line

6" (or larger) drafting triangle

Omnigrid ruler

Straight pins

Stock-size foam core board that measures 40" x 48" or 40" x 60" (I like the larger size). It should be ½" thick; any thinner and it will bend. These boards are available at craft and art supply stores.

Once you have the necessary supplies, it will take about twenty minutes to mark a 2¼" diagonal grid on the flannel. The grid will enable you to work in more than one area at a time, and it will help to keep the sewing rows straight.

STEP 1   Press the flannel and secure it to the foam core board with three or four pins. Place the 6" drafting triangle on the upper right-hand corner of the flannel board with the two shorter sides running parallel to the top and right perimeters. Draw a line along the longest edge of the 6" drafting triangle.

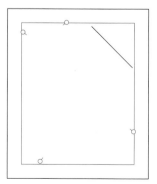

STEP 2   Remove the triangle. Now you have established the first 45° angle line.

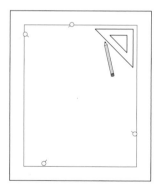

STEP 3 Using the ruler and pencil, draw a second diagonal line that measures a 2¼" distance from the first line.

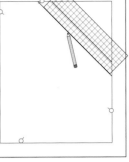

STEP 4 Using the ruler and pencil, draw diagonal lines that measure 2¼" apart, across the surface of the flannel. Continue drawing lines until you reach the lower left-hand corner.

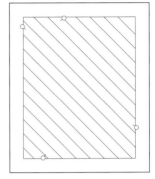

STEP 5 To make the diagonal lines in the opposite direction, move the ruler to the upper left-hand corner and place it in the opposite direction of the pencil lines that are already drawn. Line up the 2¼" increment marks on the ruler with the pencil lines on the flannel. Draw a diagonal line.

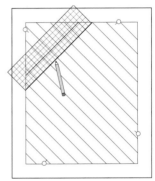

STEP 6 Continue drawing diagonal lines that measure 2¼" apart, across the surface of the flannel until you reach the lower right-hand corner. Put more pins around the perimeter of the flannel to firmly attach it to the foam core board.

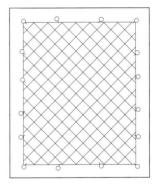

Now you have a perfectly lovely design board with a 2¼" diagonal-grid surface that is a replica of the blank Diagonal Grid shown on page 70. The squares of fabric will adhere to the flannel without the need for pinning. The design board can be leaned against the wall or a sturdy chair. One of the advantages of this board is that it's portable, giving you the opportunity to move your design from room to room to examine it in a different light.

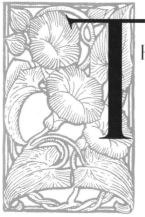

THE DESIGN PROCESS

A good cook uses only the freshest ingredients to make a culinary masterpiece, but when the necessary ingredients aren't readily available, he or she has to do a little creative improvising. This "make-do" philosophy can also be applied to fabric selection. I love working with new fabrics but when I started making Impressionist Landscapes, I was surprised to learn that floral prints are seasonal. Can you imagine? For some reason they're more available in the spring and summer. So during the times of the year when florals are scarce, I'm forced to do a little creative improvising of my own. In the winter of 1995, there were some gorgeous water textures available so I took advantage of these "fresh ingredients" and made several landscapes focusing on water instead of flowers. The point I'm trying to make is this: When you can't find the right prints for a current project, improvise. Simply alter the pattern to fit the available fabrics. To help you, I've suggested improvisational changes for each of the six projects.

DESIGN SUGGESTIONS

The time you spend making an Impressionist Landscape should be as pleasant as possible, so here are some suggestions that will make your design decisions easier.

Always work in the best possible light; natural daylight if possible. If you design at night, be consistent about working on the project during the evening hours. Colors change dramatically under artificial lighting. What looks good to you at night may not harmonize with your daytime designing and you could be working at cross purposes.

Gradually, as you work with the flower squares, your ability to blend a greater variety of colors and fabrics will grow. Floral prints that look at first like they won't work, might blend perfectly when there are more squares on your design board.

Don't labor too long in one area. If some squares aren't doing what you want them to do, leave them in place for the time being and continue designing. You can make revisions later when your landscape is further along and you have a clearer understanding of what you want it to look like.

The 2¼" base square is the "work horse" square. Many of my landscapes are made entirely with this size. When I choose to include larger squares and rectangles,

I always put some 2¼" squares near them to make the blending look more natural. You will find an example of how this is accomplished on page 82.

Make an effort to keep the design rows straight while you work; it will be much easier to sew the rows together later on.

If you have trouble following a Master Diagram, try positioning a square of fabric on the design board and then mark, or shade, the corresponding square on the Master Diagram. This method will be particularly helpful when you are working on the *The Incredible Flowering Tree* project.

If a new flower or element print is introduced and it looks too bright, flip the fabric over to the reverse side and try it again.

Every floral fabric that is introduced into the design should be repeated in at least two other squares. Using just one square from a floral fabric will make it look as though it doesn't belong.

Don't spend fifteen minutes staring at a fabric wondering if it will work. It only takes a few seconds to cut out a square and try it.

Use a reducing glass to check the blending of value and color from one area to another. A reducing glass is just the opposite of a magnifying glass. It gives you the feeling that you're standing at least ten feet away from your quilt. It helps you spot any errors in your design or flowers that stand out too much. If a square (or squares) looks like an unintentional focus, it should be changed.

When you become physically tired, stop. If you continue cutting out squares and designing, you will probably start making mistakes.

Before sewing your landscape, live with it for awhile. Look at it during different times of the day and keep trying to improve it.

It's never too late to change a square. Even after the quilt top is sewn, you can still pick out any offending squares and replace them. Sometimes I spend more time picking out and fixing than designing and sewing.

Finally, try not to be disappointed if your first effort doesn't live up to your expectations. My advice would be to say to yourself, "This is the best I can do now—the next one will be better!"

Fifth Season, 1996, 42" x 43", Gai Perry

ADDITIONAL DESIGN TECHNIQUES

I love old quilts and in my heart I'm still a traditional quiltmaker. When I first started making Impressionist Landscape quilts, I thought of them as One-Patch or Postage Stamp quilts and my intent was to see how far I could push the creative use of fabric without resorting to any kind of embellishment. Because I know how to paint, it would have been easy to touch-up and improve a finished landscape; but, for some perverse reason, it was more of a challenge to let the fabric do all the work. I knew I was moving against current trends, which encouraged the addition of beads, buttons, and fancy stitching...but I couldn't help it, I wanted my quilts to look unadorned, like pristine little fabric paintings. This "holier than thou" attitude came to an end when I designed *Poppy Fields*. I had to use the tiniest bit of paint to suggest the upper trunk of a tree and it was very liberating! Since then, I've used paint to change the color of a flower or to whitewash the top of a hill to get a smoother transition into the sky. I work with artist acrylics and usually I do the touch-up painting after a quilt top is sewn. At that point it's much easier to decide what needs to be doctored. If you want to try any of the following paint techniques, I suggest you practice first on some extra fabric.

Painting on Fabric

Materials   Use small tubes of artist acrylic paint. You will need the six spectrum colors plus titanium white and raw umber. With these few colors and some experimentation with the color circle, you can teach yourself how to mix any color you might conceivably want. Use white to lighten a color. To darken a color, use raw umber or the complement of the color you want to darken. For example, mix in a small amount of green to darken red. You can also use small jars of Setacolor® in the same range of colors as the acrylics. Setacolor is a transparent fabric paint that is perfect for making sky and water effects. Because acrylic paint is opaque, it is a better choice for changing the color of a fabric.

Shallow glass or china containers (custard cups are good) work well for holding the paints. The advantage of using glass or china is that they can be washed and used again, even after the paint has dried. Simply soak the cups in warm water for a few minutes and peel off the softened paint.

Use two or three soft bristle brushes. I like #2, #4, and #6 brushes for detail work and a wider brush (measuring at least ¾" across the bristles) for streaking fabric.

Use a large glass of clean water for rinsing the brushes.

To lighten an area: Put a little dab of titanium-white acrylic paint in a shallow container. Add enough water to the paint to make it look like skim milk. Using a soft, artist's brush, carefully apply the paint (one square at a time) to the area you want to lighten. At first it will look too white, but as it dries it will fade into the fabric. Add more layers, if necessary, to get the desired effect. (Again, acrylic paint is a good choice for this procedure because it is opaque.) If you don't like what's happening to the fabric color, quickly scrub the paint off with a clean, wet brush. Blot with a rag or paper towel.

To lighten a black background around a flower: Occasionally, after sewing, the black background around a flower will stand out because the black is too intense. You can lighten it by following the same procedure described above.

To change the color of a flower: Decide what color you want to make the flower. Mix a small amount of the chosen acrylic color in a shallow container. Add some titanium white to lighten it, and paint the flower using one of the soft bristle brushes. *Note:* Mix the color just a little bit lighter than you think it should be because, in this instance, the paint will dry a shade darker.

To make pretty sky fabric: Select a half yard of a solid colored fabric. It could be light blue, peach, cream, rose, or whatever sky color you want. Rinse the fabric to remove any sizing. While the fabric is still wet, spread it out on a flat surface. I work on my kitchen counter, using a sheet of plastic to protect the tile. This time use the transparent Setacolor. Put a little bit of the color, or colors, you want into shallow containers. Add enough water to make the paints very thin and spreadable. Now be brave and take the wide bristle brush and put streaks of paint across the fabric. Brush on some clear water to blend and soften the colors. Allow the fabric to dry

Hand-Painted Sky Fabric

naturally. (I like to spread it on a sunny patch of grass.) As the fabric dries, the colors will mellow and you'll have some beautiful sky fabric to cut into squares. This painting method is easy and very soon you will feel quite artistic.

Patch Appliqué

Another touch-up procedure I'm using to finish a quilt top is something I call patch appliqué. When I work with a combination of square sizes, sometimes there are awkward junctures when the quilt is sewn. This is because larger squares don't blend together as gracefully as smaller squares. When one of these awkward junctures occurs, I cut out a leaf or a small flower, and appliqué it over the offending area. It's a simple but effective touch-up. *Fifth Season*, on page 66, is covered with patch appliqué.

Occasionally I need to appliqué a focus element to my finished quilt top. (There was no other way to add the bridge for the quilt shown on page 118.) Although appliqué is my least favorite "quilt thing" to do, I find that once in awhile it becomes necessary.

BEFORE

AFTER

Patch Appliqué

Diagonal Grid

GENERAL PROJECT INSTRUCTIONS

For each quilt, use the Master Diagram as a reference for the placement of squares. Each diagram is shaded to help you interpret the light, medium, and dark value areas of the individual landscapes. The blank diagonal grid on the opposite page can be used to create your own designs. It's a good idea to photocopy the grid so you can have extras on hand for doodling (refer to page 2 for photocopy permission).

Keep referring to the fabric swatches (pages 46–58) to find ideas for the appropriate use of floral and element fabrics.

The yardage requirements are, at best, an educated guess. After you have completed the first project, you will have a better idea of determining how much of each fabric to buy.

Study the quilt examples for inspiration and guidance.

Cutting the foreground flowers individually by hand is a necessity for the successful completion of a landscape.

In this book, I've divided the 2¼" base square into fourths. This small 1⅜" square allows a smoother movement from one element to another (by eliminating the sawtooth look). The smaller squares are particularly effective when used at the edge of a body of water or outlining trees and foliage. Some of the Master Diagrams indicate their use.

Don't let the patterns inhibit your creativity. Feel free to change them in order to express your personal interpretation of nature, color, and the environment.

The project information is cumulative so, if you decide to skip a project, you will miss some helpful design information.

I'm pleased to be able to share some student quilts for the first four projects. They represent a skill level that ranges from beginning quilter to advanced seamstress. I think each of the quilts is a nice example of the artist's ability to blend fabrics and express her personal palette. I haven't had the opportunity to teach the fifth and sixth projects yet, but I know you'll have fun designing *Victorian Bouquet* with all its big beautiful flowers. As for *Les Fleurs*, well just let me say, enjoy the challenge!

Land, Sea, and Sky, 1996, 37½" x 32", Gai Perry

LAND, SEA, AND SKY

The first project quilt was inspired by an early Monet painting entitled *Argenteuil, the Bank of Flowers*. Monet's original composition is far more complex than my quilt. The painting shows some buildings along the far shore, a few trees, and several people in the foreground. This simplified version of the painting becomes a gentle triad of land, sea, and sky. I selected a value-graded fabric in tones of pink, lavender, and turquoise for the water area. Notice how I put the darkest value of the water fabric along the edge of the bank and the lightest value in the middle of the water in order to suggest a reflection of light. The sky is composed of just one fabric, but the way it's arranged with the darkest value touching the horizon, one might think that more than one fabric is involved. I put some leaves along the foreground section of water to ease the transition from the water area to the flower area. The random arrangement of flowers in the foreground suggests a meadow of wildflowers. The quilt looks very impressionistic and with its predominance of cool colors, it gives the viewer a feeling of serenity.

Fabric Requirements

Use the swatches beginning on page 46 as a reference. Minimum fabric requirements are suggested, but more is always better!

SKY Choose a light value sky fabric, preferably something that is multi-hued or has an interesting gradation of color. You will need a half yard.

WATER Select one water fabric that is value graded, or two or three water fabrics in similar colors. They should be in a medium to light range of values. You will need a total amount of one yard.

LEAVES Find one or more leaf prints in a color, or colors, that will blend into the darkest value of the water. You will need a quarter yard.

FLOWERS I cut up one of the "wonder fabrics" for the flower area in the foreground. Because all the flowers on this print are rendered in a small scale, I used only the 2¼" square and its corresponding triangle. If you want to put some larger flowers in your landscape, use the larger templates. The amount of floral prints is optional.

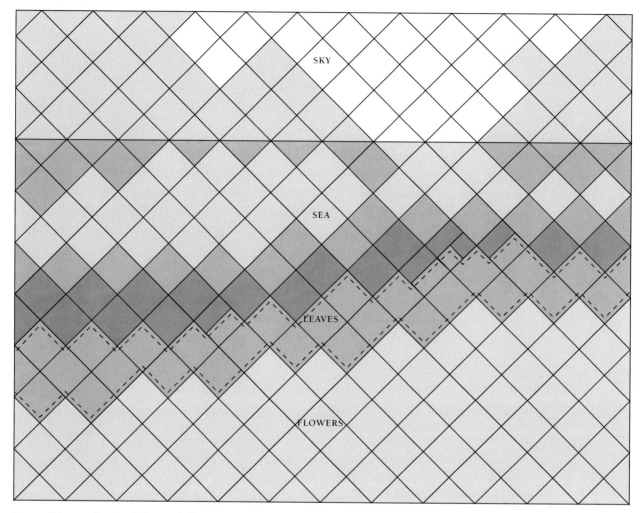

Master Diagram for *Land, Sea, and Sky*

Begin the Design

STEP 1   Cut out twelve 2⅝" triangles of water fabric and twelve 2⅝" triangles of sky fabric. The sky should be a lighter value than the water to show the contrast of the horizon. Refer to the Master Diagram and place the triangles on the flannel design board on either side of the horizon line. *Note:* Until they are sewn together, triangles take up more space than their corresponding squares. To compensate while you are designing, overlap the triangles.

STEP 2   Strip-cut the appropriate number of 2¼" water squares. Remember to cut the strips on a 45° angle if the water fabric has a printed grain that needs to run parallel to the horizon (refer to the cutting instructions on page 61.) Follow the same procedure for the sky fabric. Add the perimeter 2⅝" triangles of water and sky. Although you will probably want to do some rearranging and refining later on, leave the squares in place for now.

STEP 3   Strip-cut the appropriate number of 2¼" leaf squares. Place them on the design board. I added a couple of the smallest squares and rectangles to help blend the leaves into the water area (refer to page 83 for an illustration of how to use these small squares and rectangles). Add the perimeter leaf triangles.

STEP 4   Now for the flowers! Designing a flower area is always a trial and error process and you'll need to keep playing with the squares until you achieve a good balance of color and flower-scale variation. I suggest putting a 2¼" flower-leaf transition print beneath the leaves. This will ease the movement from the leaves to the flower area. Now is the time to mix in some larger flowers, if you have them. Remember, one 4" square takes the place of four 2¼" squares. *Note:* Until the quilt is sewn, a 4" square takes up less physical space; it won't quite fill up the space on the design board that's allotted for four 2¼" squares.

Cut out a few 2¼" squares of leaves from the floral prints and place them "here and there" to give cool contrast to the warm-colored flowers.

Dovetailing Different Fabrics

Tip on Arranging Floral Squares: As you move from one floral fabric to another, try not to create diagonal lines and obvious divisions. Instead, dovetail the floral fabrics as shown in the example. The overall effect will be more natural looking.

When all the flower squares are in place, add the perimeter flower triangles. Now it's time to fine tune your design. Move several feet away (or use your reducing glass), and ask yourself the following questions:

Fine-Tuning Checklist

Is the sky the lightest value?

Does the water have movement, and does it look liquid?

Is there a nice color relationship between the water and the sky?

Do the leaves blend into the water and flowers without hard edges?

Are the flowers colorful enough, and are the different floral fabrics artfully blended?

When you are comfortable with your design, it's time to sew. Turn to page 109 for the finishing instructions.

Improvisations

If you can't find suitable water fabrics, eliminate the water element and plant a meadow that extends all the way to the horizon. Flowers at the back of the meadow should be smaller and in lighter values to suggest distance.

Sometimes realistic leaf prints can be almost impossible to find. An acceptable substitute would be a flower-leaf transition of prints in a color that blends into the water.

Moorea Bay,
1996, 35" x 41",
Pamela Stringer

Asilomar: Monterey County,
1996, 36" x 31",
Judy Howlett

The Incredible Flowering Tree, 1996, 32" x 39½", Gai Perry

THE INCREDIBLE FLOWERING TREE

In 1992 I made an Impressionist Landscape quilt that looked like a semi-abstract version of a leafy tree with flowers growing around the base. It's a nice quilt, but whenever someone takes a picture of it, they invariably turn the photo upside down. Instead of a leafy tree, it looks like a tree in full bloom. Since that seemed to be the consensus of opinion, I thought, Why not?, and I designed *The Incredible Flowering Tree*. The first time I taught the quilt in a workshop, a student announced, "I'm not going to put any flowers in my tree, just leaves!" (Sometimes you just can't win, but I liked her interpretation of the pattern. It is shown on page 85.)

This quilt is pure fantasy, so let your imagination run wild. There are at least seven varieties of flowers blooming among the leaves, and the effect, though not realistic, is very pretty. The tree sits in the foreground of a flowering meadow and its crown is framed by a pale blue and blue-green sky. The quilt projects a feeling of strong contrasts because of the hard-edge trunk and the fact that the crown of the tree stands boldly in front of the sky rather than blending into it.

Fabric Requirements

SKY The sky can be any color that pleases you. It doesn't have to blend into the crown of the tree or be in the same color family as the meadow. You will need a half yard.

TREE TRUNK Look for a dark value print that suggests the bark of a tree. You will need an eighth yard.

CROWN FLOWERS I've combined 2¼" and 4" squares with a few 4" rectangles to give a nice variety of flower sizes. Look for floral prints that have interesting leaves. You will need a half yard each of at least five prints.

MEADOW FLOWERS *Foreground*—Find three floral prints in colors that are compatible with the crown flowers. Since the crown flowers are the focus of this landscape, the flowers in the foreground should be smaller and less showy. You will need quarter yard pieces of each.
Mid-Distance—Refer to the meadow fabric swatches on page 49. Select one or two smaller scale floral prints in colors that reflect the foreground flowers. You will need quarter yard pieces of each.
Far-Distance—I used an interesting texture (on the reverse side) for the far-distance flowers. You can use a texture, or one or two small-scale floral prints for a similar effect. You will need a total of a half yard.

Master Diagram for *The Incredible Flowering Tree*

Begin the Design

STEP 1   Since the flowers in the crown of the tree are the main focus and will determine the color scheme for the rest of the quilt, you will arrange these first. Select several floral prints that appear to look compatible. (If you need to refresh your memory on compatibility of prints, refer to page 45.) Because this tree is a product of your imagination, you can combine an impossible variety of flowers. Iris, roses, tulips, big flowers, little flowers—the more the merrier! Cut two or three flowers from each print and place them in the upper center of the design board, as shown in the example. This is just a temporary arrangement allowing you to become familiar with the flowers you've selected. Let your instinct guide you. If you think a flower looks jarring, or out of place, discard it and select another. When you have a group of flowers that looks promising, remove the squares from the board and start the actual design.

Temporary Crown Arrangement

STEP 2   Place the first flower square in a position that corresponds to the space marked on the Master Diagram with an x. Put a pin in the square as a marker to help you count rows. Start adding flowers and continue until the crown area of the tree is complete.

In a landscape where you are combining different size squares and rectangles, it is important to arrange some 2¼" squares near the larger squares and rectangles. The placement of smaller squares makes the larger ones look more believable. The reasoning is simple: The smaller the square, the easier it is to blend different fabrics together. The first example shows four 4" squares grouped together and even though only one fabric is involved, the junctures look awkward. The second example shows two 4" squares and an equivalent amount of 2¼" squares plus a rectangle. The blend looks more realistic because of the addition of smaller scale squares.

If you study the crown of my tree, you will notice that most of the squares around the edge, and directly above the trunk, are executed with leaves. Also, I've used tiny squares and rectangles "here and there", at the edge of the crown, to create a more graceful shape.

WRONG

RIGHT

Blending Different Square Sizes

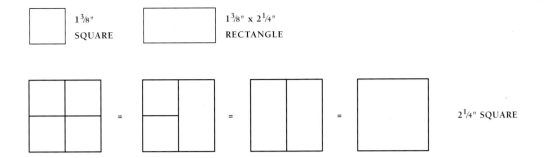

$1\frac{3}{8}$"
SQUARE

$1\frac{3}{8}$" x $2\frac{1}{4}$"
RECTANGLE

$2\frac{1}{4}$" SQUARE

Combinations of Smaller Squares and Rectangles Can Equal a $2\frac{1}{4}$" Square

STEP 3 Cut and place the $2\frac{1}{4}$" squares and $2\frac{5}{8}$" triangles for the tree trunk. You will find this very satisfying because it anchors the flowers, which until now have been floating in mid-air.

STEP 4 Add the $2\frac{1}{4}$" and $1\frac{3}{8}$" squares, the $1\frac{3}{8}$" x $2\frac{1}{4}$" rectangles, and the perimeter $2\frac{5}{8}$" triangles for the sky and the horizon line.

STEP 5 Now you can start filling in the meadow. Cut nine $2\frac{5}{8}$" triangles from the far-distance meadow floral print (or texture) and place them along the horizon line. Using the Master Diagram as a guide, work down to the foreground flowers. Try turning the squares over to the reverse side to get a smoother blend from one fabric to another. When all the meadow squares are in place, add the perimeter $2\frac{5}{8}$" triangles.

Fine-Tuning Checklist

Is the sky the lightest value?

Is the crown of the tree the main focus, or do the flowers in the foreground have too much importance?

Does the tree trunk look too dark or too light?

Is the meadow believable? Do you get a feeling of distance?

Are the flowers in the crown of the tree beautifully integrated, which means do they blend into each other?

Improvisations

I've noticed that sometimes the textured fabric a student selects for the far-distance meadow area turns out to look more like a water fabric. If this happens to you, eliminate the mid-distance flowers and continue with the water texture fabric until you get to the foreground flowers. The tree will look like it's standing on a gentle slope overlooking a body of water.

Imagine This,
1996, 33" x 40",
Cheron Adrian

In the Pink,
1996, 12" x 16",
Barbara Keeton

Barbara used the tiny 1⅜" square to
create this charming miniature tree quilt.

Juin,
1996, 39" x 45¾",
Pamela Creason

Monet's Garden IV, 1996, 40½" x 33½", Gai Perry

MONET'S GARDEN

I received so many pattern requests for the *Monet's Garden* quilt in *Impressionist Quilts* that I didn't dare write this book without including instructions. The scene depicts the path (the Grande Allée) that runs from Monet's house to the gate at the front of his property. If you could somehow open the gate, you'd be able to walk across the road and enjoy a view of his famous lily pond. I've made four versions of this quilt and in the first three I lined the path with the same colors of nasturtiums and roses he'd planted so many years ago. For this quilt, I devised my own landscape plan, which focuses on some bright red-orange geraniums and several kinds of informal small-scale flowers. I've grouped some leafy prints on either side of the gate posts to suggest a hedge framing the garden. The overall impression is one of sunlight and summer flowers.

Fabric Requirements

SKY Look for a sky texture in a color gradation that will blend into the leafy hedge without creating too sharp a distinction of color and value. You will need a half yard.

GATE The real gate in Monet's garden is painted blue-green so I used a blue-green tone-on-tone print. In retrospect, I think the gate would be more effective if it were rendered in a warm color, such as a rosy red or maybe even a wood-grained fabric. You will need an eighth yard.

GATE POSTS Find a fabric print that contrasts with the gate and the hedge color. Brick or stone would be interesting. You will need an eighth yard.

HEDGE The hedge is the darkest value element in this landscape. Find one or two small-scale leafy prints from the same color family. Purchase quarter yard pieces of each.

PATH Select one path print. I used a lightweight decorator fabric that gives the impression of sunlight and shadow. Often a light background floral print used on the reverse side will work perfectly. You will need a half yard.

TRANSITION Choose one or two flower-leaf transition prints to line the path. They should be in colors that will blend into the path, as well as into the flowers.

FOREGROUND I've used four $4\frac{3}{8}$" triangles of red, yellow, and pink roses in the left foreground. Otherwise, all the flowers fit into the $2\frac{1}{4}$" square. The foreground is filled with a mass planting of geraniums. Pansies would also be attractive. Refer to Flowers that Grow in Masses for $2\frac{1}{4}$" Squares on page 48 for ideas. The amounts are optional.

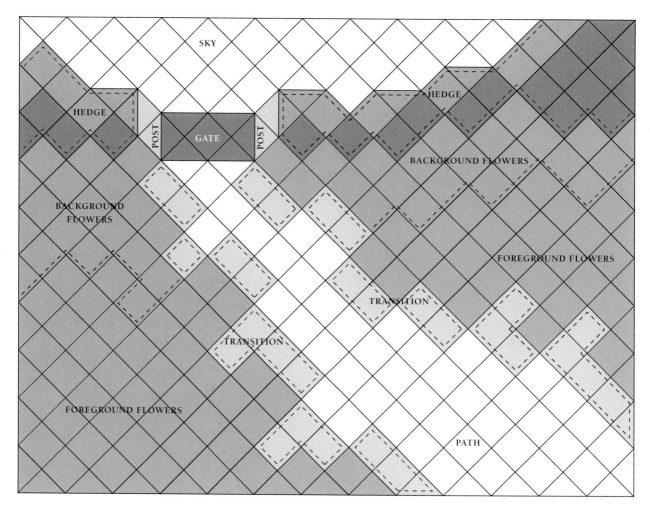

Master Diagram for *Monet's Garden*

BACKGROUND To help ease the transition into the small-scale flowers, put a few individual flowers for 2¼" squares behind the mass planting in the foreground. I used petite roses. Fill the rear of the garden with some small-scale meadow-style flowers. Notice how I arranged the little white flowers to act as a border along the front of the hedge. The amounts are optional.

Begin the Design

STEP 1 Rotary-cut the appropriate number of 2¼" path squares and place them on the design board. Decide whether the front or the reverse side of the fabric looks better. Perhaps you will end up using the fabric both ways, putting the lighter reverse side in the middle of the path. Add two 2⅝" triangles to form the top of the path and five 2⅝" triangles along the right foreground and side perimeter.

STEP 2 Using the Master Diagram as a reference, line both sides of the path with the transition fabrics. Remember, they must be in a color, or colors, that will visually blend into the path and also into the flower areas. Again, decide if the transition prints create a better blend if they're used on the reverse side wherever they touch a path square.

RIGHT

WRONG

Blending the Path Fabric into the Transition Fabric

STEP 3 Now you're ready to plant the garden. You will have to use your judgment when deciding how to cut the flowers (individually or strip-cut). Start in the foreground and work toward the hedge. Remember to integrate the different floral prints by dovetailing the squares. An example of dovetailing is shown on page 76. Monet planted his path in a symmetrical arrangement (the same flowers on either side) and I think this arrangement creates a nice balance. Using my quilt as a reference, add the smaller background flowers after the larger foreground flowers are in place. Then add the 2⅝" perimeter triangles.

STEP 4 Cut one 2¼" square and six 2⅝" triangles from the gate fabric and position them in their correct location on the design board. Refer to the Master Diagram for placement. Cut four 2⅝" gate post triangles and place them on either side of the gate.

STEP 5 Rotary strip-cut some 2¼" squares of the small-scale leaf prints and build the hedge along the back of the garden. Notice that I've used some 2⅝" triangles to break up the line of the hedge as it moves into the sky fabric. Add the perimeter 2⅝" hedge triangles.

STEP 6 Finally, rotary strip-cut the 2¼" squares for the sky. Add the 2⅝" sky triangles.

Fine-Tuning Checklist

Do the sky and the path read as the lightest value?

Is the gate believable? Does the gate color have a nice relationship to the rest of the landscape?

Does the transition fabric blend smoothly into the path?

Are the flowers on either side of the path arranged gracefully and symmetrically?

Do the flowers project an overall blur of color? Use the reducing glass to check your design. If any squares jump out, replace them.

Improvisations

Here again, sometimes the path fabric will end up looking like a flowing stream. If it does, and you like the effect, go with it and replace the gate and gate posts with even smaller meadow flowers to give the viewer a sense of distance.

If you can't find small-scale leaf fabrics for the hedge, use three tone-on-tone prints in shades that are compatible with the other greens in your landscape. For example, if most of the leaves in your flower squares are a blue-green hue, use blue-green tone-on-tone prints for the hedge.

Whispers in Lavender,
1996, 40" x 32",
Katherine Cavanaugh

In the Garden,
1996, 41" x 34",
Barbara Keeton

Serendipity,
1996, 41" x 34",
Terése May

Field and Stream, 1996, 33" x 41", Gai Perry

FIELD AND STREAM

After I painted *Poppy Fields,* I started another picture. Before it was finished, though, I was pulled back to quilting and the painting has been sitting on a shelf ever since. When I was trying to come up with a more complicated design for the fourth project, I remembered the composition of the painting and I thought it would be a good subject for a landscape quilt.

There are several natural elements in this landscape. A bed of brightly colored iris is planted along either side of a flowing stream. Behind the iris, a grassy meadow meanders toward a grove of trees. Above the trees there is a majestic range of mountains that reach into the sky, and even I'm not sure where the mountains stop and the sky begins.

Fabric Requirements

SKY   Like the other projects, the sky is once again the lightest value in the landscape. Unless the sky is the focus of a composition, I like to keep it simple by using just one fabric. Choose one or two fabrics that will blend into the lightest color of the mountains. You will need a total of a half yard.

MOUNTAINS   Two or three tone-on-tone and color-dominant prints are needed to suggest the texture of mountains. They should also be graded from a medium-dark value to a light value that is almost indistinguishable from the sky fabric. I think I was lucky to find a light-colored fabric that looks like snow caps. You will need a quarter yard of each.

TREES   I used a textured fabric to give the appearance of a growth of trees at the back of the meadow. Look for a tone-on-tone fabric that has a mottled character (one that projects a feeling of sunlight on tree tops). You will need a half yard.

GRASSY MEADOW   Find one tone-on-tone print in a medium-value fabric that looks like grass. You will need a half yard.

FLOWERS   I love the effect of the iris growing along the stream. There are several iris fabrics available now but if you can't find any, consider daffodils or maybe some brilliant red or yellow tulips. You will probably need a whole yard. Also, you will need a quarter yard of a small-scale flower-leaf print to help blend the flowers into the meadow.

Master Diagram for *Field and Stream*

TRANSITION   I've placed a long-bladed grass print along the far side of the water. The green color helps to soften the edge of the river bank and ease the movement into the flowers. An appropriately colored flower-leaf transition print would also do the job. You will need a quarter yard.

STREAM   Look for some tone-on-tone prints or a value-graded print that will give the illusion of flowing water. You will need a total of one yard.

Begin the Design

STEP 1   Cut the 2¼" water squares and place them in the correct position on the design board. Put the lightest value squares in the center of the stream. Notice that I used a few of the smaller squares and rectangles to make the bank appear irregular. You may or may not need to do this. Add the perimeter 2⅝" water triangles.

STEP 2   Arrange the foreground flowers. They will need to be cut individually. I used the 2¼" square and the 2¼" x 4" rectangle. Add the perimeter floral triangles.

STEP 3   Cut the 2¼" transition squares and place them along the far bank of the stream. Now add the flowers that are growing on the far side of the stream and make them look similar to the flowers that you planted on the near side of the stream. Sprinkle some squares of the small-scale flower-leaf print behind them and then add the grass squares. Referring to the Master Diagram, cut seven 2⅝" triangles to help define where the grass stops and the trees begin. Add the perimeter grass triangles.

STEP 4   Cut a combination of squares and triangles from the darkest area of the tree fabric and place them directly above the grass triangles. Add the rest of the 2¼" tree squares. Cut them individually so that you can get darker value squares to put near the grass and lighter value squares to put near the mountains. Add the perimeter tree triangles.

STEP 5   Build the mountains. There is no formula for this, other than to start with the darkest value print and move toward the lightest value print. It will be another trial and error process until the rhythm and balance of the mountains feel right. The lightest value mountain fabric should fade into the sky fabric. Add the perimeter mountain triangles.

STEP 6   Add the 2¼" sky squares and the perimeter sky triangles.

Fine-Tuning Checklist

Are the mountains blending softly into the sky?

Do the trees fade into the mountains?

Do you like the way the flowers are arranged?

Does your water fabric really look like a flowing stream?

Improvisations

If you have trouble finding the right water fabric, turn the stream into a path.

If you can't figure out how to blend the mountains into the sky, give them a hard-edge look by making the mountains a distinctly darker value than the sky. Refer to the Alternate Diagram for Hard-Edge Mountains.

The grassy style of meadow can be eliminated. Use meadow flowers instead.

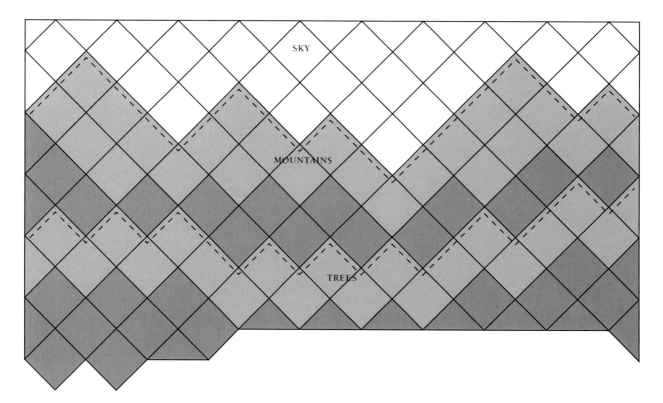

Alternate Diagram for Hard-Edge Mountains

Pieceful Valley,
1996, 35" x 40",
Billie Shewey

After the Storm,
1996, 31" x 38",
Katherine Cavanaugh

Victorian Bouquet, 1996, 25" x 26½", Gai Perry

VICTORIAN BOUQUET

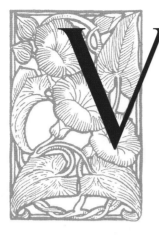

It took me a long time to get up the nerve to attempt a "still life." I wasn't sure it was possible to do something like this with just squares. The project seemed like it might be more suited to an appliqué technique, but to my utter amazement it worked, and this is one of my favorite quilts. My concept was to design an opulent bouquet and place it in front of a busy Victorian floral wallpaper. I wanted the flowers to fade in and out of the background, like an impressionist painting. I didn't plan a color scheme, but I knew if I kept adding more and more flowers the result would be overstated…and very Victorian. The other bouquet quilt, *Vase with White Roses* (page 4), is a perfect example of an analogous color scheme. It was made with just three fabrics: the flowers, the background, and the vase. The floral print is a lovely painterly looking fabric that would be difficult to blend with other flowers because it's so distinctive. *Victorian Bouquet* is a good example of a controlled color scheme.

Fabric Requirements

FLOWERS   Try to find one or two "wonder print" florals that have flowers suitable for the 2¼" and 4" squares. You will also want to add a few more florals just to jar the color scheme a bit. If the flowers are too compatible, the bouquet could end up looking dull. It's also important to choose floral prints that have attractive leaves. Amounts are optional.

TRANSITION   This fabric will help to blend the flowers into the background. Look for a small-scale floral in colors that are slightly darker than the background print. You will need a quarter yard.

BACKGROUND   I found a large-scale painterly looking floral for *Victorian Bouquet*. I used the print on the reverse side above the flowers and on the front side beneath the flowers to give some subtle shading. For the *Vase with White Roses* (page 4), I chose a contemporary looking leaf print in the same analogous color scheme as the flowers. You will need one yard.

VASE   Try to get an interesting tie-dye, batik, or two-tone texture that will give a feeling of light reflection. You will need a quarter yard.

BACKGROUND

TRANSITION

X

FLOWERS

BACKGROUND

VASE

BACKGROUND

Master Diagram for *Victorian Bouquet*

The Master Diagram has been altered slightly so the quilt will fit on your design board.

Begin the Design

STEP 1 Start designing the bouquet following the same procedure you used for the crown section of *The Incredible Flowering Tree* (page 81). First, create a temporary arrangement of compatible flowers. When you've selected the floral prints you want to use, remove the squares from the board and start the actual design.

STEP 2 I found it easier to start at the top center of the bouquet. Choose a nice showy flower that fills a 4" square and place it in the large square marked with the x. Add some more 4" flower squares as indicated on the Master Diagram. Continue placing small-, medium-, and large-scale flowers on your design board until the flower area is filled. Template size is optional. Notice the orientation of the flowers; some of them droop sideways and downward, just like a real bouquet. Also notice how I've placed leaves from the floral prints along the lower edge of the bouquet. Pay attention to how the different size squares and rectangles are lining up. If they don't conform to a diagonal sewing-row pattern, either adjust some squares or look at the next project, *Les Fleurs*, to learn how to sew in units rather than in rows.

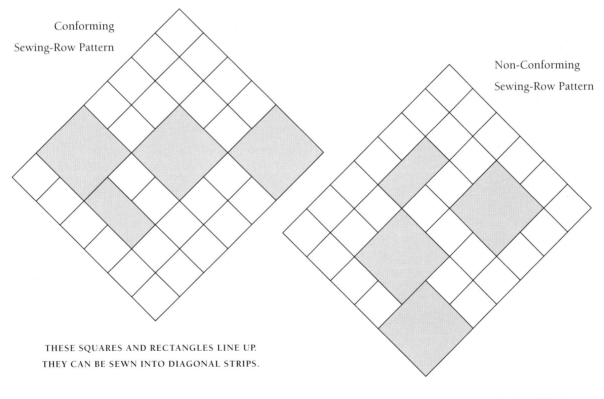

Conforming
Sewing-Row Pattern

Non-Conforming
Sewing-Row Pattern

THESE SQUARES AND RECTANGLES LINE UP.
THEY CAN BE SEWN INTO DIAGONAL STRIPS.

THESE SQUARES AND RECTANGLES OVERLAP.
THEY MUST BE SEWN INTO SEPARATE UNITS.

STEP 3 Put some 2¼" squares of the transition print across the top of the bouquet as indicated on the Master Diagram.

STEP 4 Design the base with 2¼" squares and 2⅝" triangles. Use your imagination to create a reflection of light.

STEP 5 Add the background squares and triangles.

Fine-Tuning Checklist

Is the vase believable?

Are the flowers arranged gracefully?

Does the bouquet blend into the background?

Improvisations

If you can't find the right fabric for the vase, try using a pictorial print of some kind (perhaps a blue and white Delft pattern).

Try designing a lavish bowl of fruit instead of flowers, or have some fun combining fruits, flowers, and vegetables.

Change the shape of the bowl and make the bouquet stand out in hard-edge relief against the background. This is accomplished by using the smallest squares and rectangles to define the shape. The transition flowers can be eliminated. Refer to the Alternate Diagram for Vase and Hard-Edge Flower Arrangement.

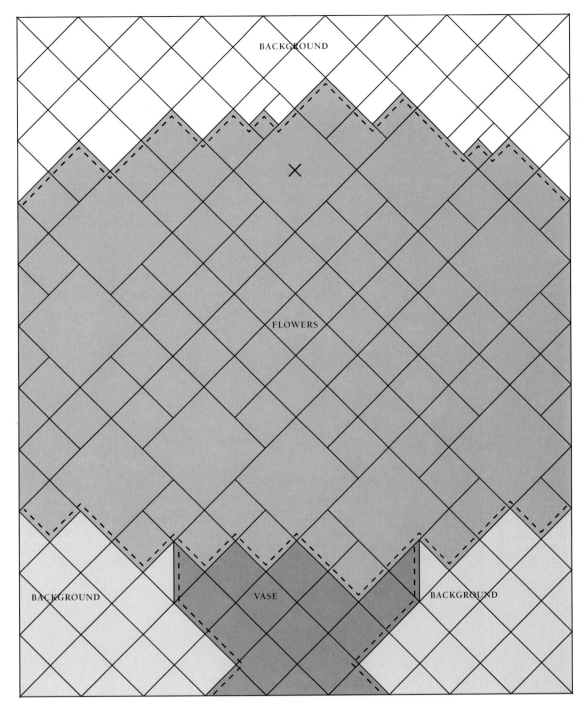

BACKGROUND

FLOWERS

BACKGROUND

VASE

BACKGROUND

Alternate Diagram for Vase and Hard-Edge Flower Arrangement

Les Fleurs, 1996, 31" x 33½", Gai Perry

LES FLEURS

Sometimes the combined color of one or two floral prints will look pretty enough to inspire me to cut some 2¼" and 4" squares. I'll group them on my design board and usually I don't have anything in mind to begin with—I just want to see how the flowers interact. If I like what's happening, I'll add more floral fabrics and gradually develop something called a "flower collage." These pieces aren't true landscapes, but rather a nice arrangement of flowers that suggests a small section of garden in full bloom. Collages are fun to design, but you need to have some interesting combinations of flowers to make them work.

As you study the project quilt, you'll notice that I broke my most important rule, which is *Never Put Floral Prints with Light and Dark Backgrounds in the Same Quilt.* I was able to make the fabrics work, in this instance, because I found that I'd purchased the rose and lilac fabric in two different colorways. One has a black background and the other a pale robin's egg blue. (A colorway means the exact same pattern executed with different colors.)

I cut some roses and lilacs from the lighter background floral and arranged them at the top of the quilt to suggest sky. Then I switched to the black background roses and lilacs and mixed them with other dark background flowers for the main body of the collage. Combining different colorways in the same quilt can be very effective. The water in the *Lily Pond Bridge II* quilt (page 118) was made with two colorways of a value-graded texture. Together they give a nice shimmer to the water.

It's going to be impossible to tell you exactly how to design this quilt because the fabrics you put together will dictate the size of the squares and where you place them. Putting the quilt together will also be a challenge because it has to be sewn into units rather than diagonal rows. If you are a novice quilter, it might be better to save this project for a later date.

The Master Diagram indicates the general outline of the flowers against the sky and suggests the movement of light to dark values. You will have to fill in the blanks.

Fabric Requirements

FLOWERS Look for a fabric with flowers that will fit in the 2¼" and 4" squares. Here's the hard part: It must be available in a dark and a light background colorway. The light color doesn't necessarily have to be blue—it could be pink for a sunset sky or yellow for a hazy summer sky. You will also need additional floral fabrics. I put some wisteria growing up the left side and some darker value, violet-type flowers spreading along the lower edge. The lavender and purple make a nice contrast with the pink roses. I also found a compatible smaller scale floral (similar to a transition print) and tucked

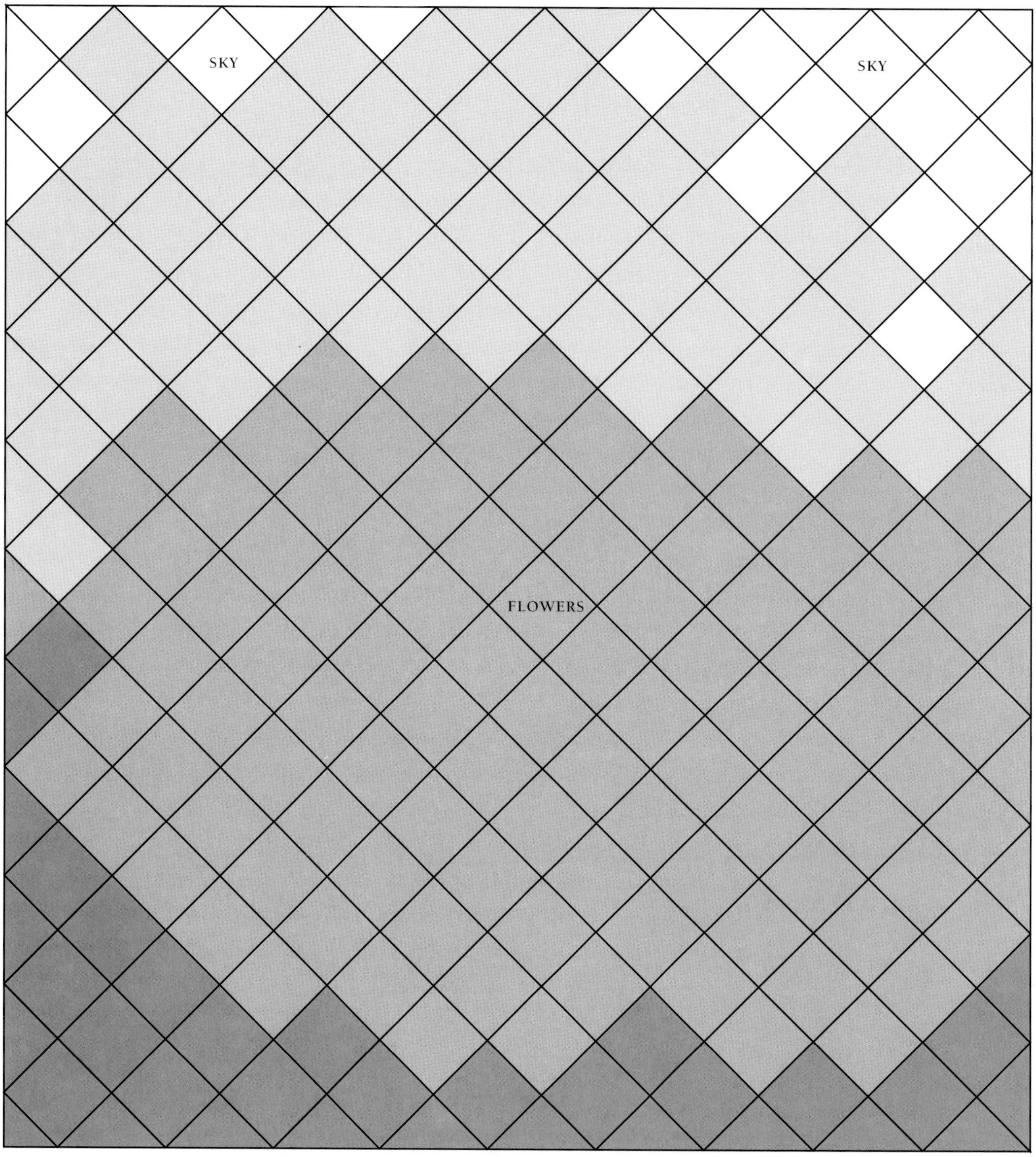
SKY
SKY
FLOWERS

Master Diagram for *Les Fleurs*

it "here and there" among the larger flowers. The yardage amount of these fabrics is optional.

Begin the Design

STEP 1   Cut some 2¼" and 4" flower squares from the lighter colorway fabric and start placing them near the top of the design board. Keep rearranging squares until the flowers look like they are growing naturally. Cut some 2¼" squares that just show the background of the light colorway fabric and place them in the sky area, as indicated in the Master Diagram. Add the perimeter sky triangles.

STEP 2   Cut some 2¼" and 4" flowers from the dark colorway fabric and arrange them directly below the light colorway flowers. Now you can work down to the foreground, mixing in large and small flowers from other fabrics. As you work, keep in mind the following design suggestions:

Mix the scale of the flowers.

Introduce a nice contrast of warm-cool colors.

Put darker value flowers at the bottom of the quilt to create a shadow effect.

Don't cut all the flowers to grow upward exactly. They will look more natural if some of them slant to the left or right.

Use some 2¼" leaf squares "here and there" for contrast.

STEP 3   When you're happy with the arrangement, it's time to figure out how to sew it together. Because of all the different sizes of squares (and possibly rectangles), it is impossible to sew diagonal strips. The photographs show how I had to sew the squares into units. Each quilt will have a different unit pattern, which will be determined by the position of the squares.

A   B   C

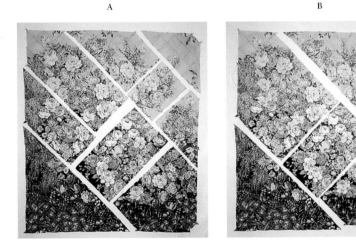 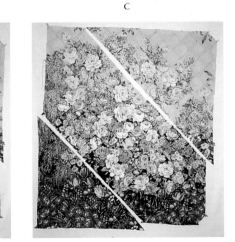

Sewing in Units

Fine-Tuning Checklist

Do the flowers blend together nicely?

Is the sky believable?

Are the flowers at the top rendered in lighter values than those at the bottom?

Improvisations

If you can't find a floral print in both a light and dark colorway, try to make-do without them. Use flowers from a light-value print for the sky and the top flower section. Find a floral print with a darker background and similar flowers, and use it to blend into the rest of the garden.

Another solution would be to use floral prints with consistently light backgrounds to design the whole piece.

SEWING THE LANDSCAPE

When I finished designing my first Impressionist Landscape, I looked at all the carefully arranged squares and triangles and I thought to myself, how in the world am I going to get this thing together? I knew that first I'd have to sew the squares into diagonal strips…but how to maintain the correct order and orientation of the flowers was a mystery. To further add to the confusion, some of the squares were used on the reverse side. The solution I came up with is not only foolproof, it's also the quickest method you'll ever learn for joining rows of squares.

EQUIPMENT

Sewing machine

Medium gray 100% cotton sewing machine thread

Pins

Scissors

Seam ripper

Note: Before sewing the squares into diagonal strips, all the opposing triangles (for example, those along the horizon line) and the smallest squares and rectangles (if you've used them) must be sewn into 2¼" squares using a ¼" seam allowance.

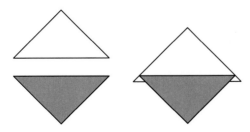

Joining 2¼" Triangles
(After sewing, trim off the overlapping points.)

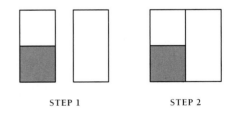

STEP 1   STEP 2

Joining Small Squares and Rectangles

METHOD FOR JOINING SQUARES

My method for joining squares and triangles works for rows where there are three or more squares. You are going to sew the squares and triangles into diagonal strips using a ¼" seam allowance. Begin sewing at the lower left-hand corner of the design and work toward the upper right-hand corner. Refer to the Sewing Diagram.

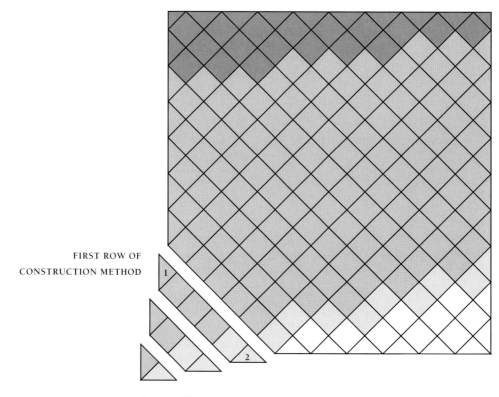

FIRST ROW OF
CONSTRUCTION METHOD

Sewing Diagram

STEP 1 Starting with the first row of the construction method, sew the upper edge triangle (1) to the square sitting diagonally below it. With the pressure foot still down, sew a few more stitches and leave the unit in the machine.

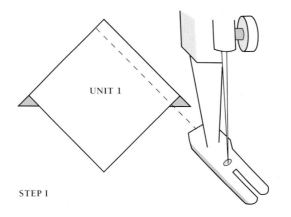

UNIT 1

STEP I

STEP 2 From the same row, pick up the lower edge triangle (2) plus the square sitting diagonally above it and sew them together. With the pressure foot still down, sew a few more
stitches and leave this unit in the machine. With your scissors, detach Unit 1.

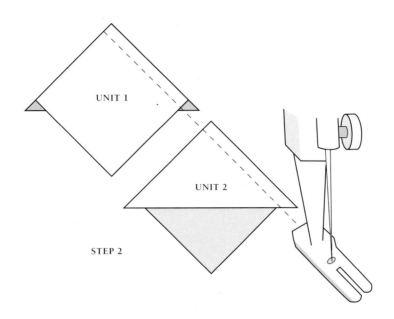

STEP 3 Move back to the top of the row and pick up the next square in the sequence. Sew it to
Unit 1. With the pressure foot still down, sew a few more stitches and then leave this
unit in the machine. With your scissors, detach Unit 2.

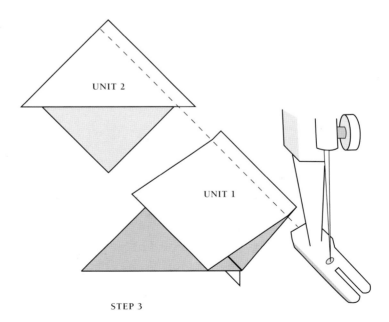

STEP 4 Move down to the lower end of the row and pick up the next square in the sequence. Sew it to Unit 2. Now with the pressure foot still down, sew a few more stitches and leave this unit in the machine.

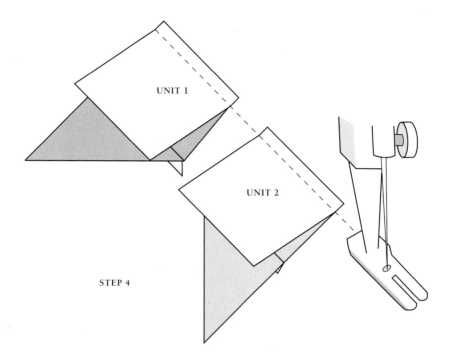

STEP 5 Continue sewing in this manner until all the squares in the row are joined to the first or second units. Sew the two units together and pin the resulting strip onto the design board in the correct position.

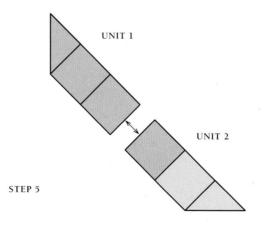

The infallibility of this method will become apparent as you continue joining the squares to the first and second units. The color areas at either end of the row will be so different that you will have no trouble figuring out which square comes next. If you lose your concentration and sew a square to the wrong unit, it will be immediately obvious because the colors won't blend and the square will look out of place. Also, each square goes into the machine with the correct orientation, leaving no opportunity to second-guess which way is supposed to be up.

In rows where there are one or more large squares, two single rows must be joined together before adding them to the larger squares.

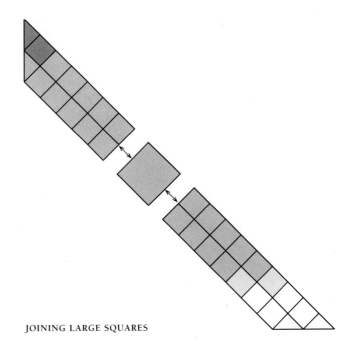

JOINING LARGE SQUARES

JOINING THE ROWS AND PRESSING

Press the seam allowances for each row in one direction only and alternate the direction from row to row. For example, if the first row is pressed toward the left, press the second row toward the right and the third row again to the left.

To join the individual rows, start in the lower left-hand corner. Pin the first row to the second row at the opposing seam allowances. Sew the two rows together. Continue joining the rows in this manner. Press all the seam allowances in the same direction, either up or down.

I've already mentioned that I'm an avid collector. This antique schoolmaster's desk sits in my living room and every few months I change the assortment of treasures that fill its cubbyholes. At Christmas, I decorate it with antique Santa Claus figures, old toys, and tree ornaments. Right now it holds an eclectic group of "found objects." When I add to my collection, it's usually because I perceive the item to be beautiful, have intrinsic value, or a funny personality…like the silly duck decoy posed in front of the quilt. My favorite pieces are the two-faced art nouveau flower vase and the handmade rag doll I found at a flea market. The copper tea kettle sitting on the desk is very old. It belonged to my husband's grandmother.

BORDERS

I've made more than fifty Impressionist Landscapes quilts but I must tell you I still experience a momentary sense of loss right after a quilt is sewn. It looks better because the unwanted seam allowances are gone, but it's so much smaller! I know each square is going to lose half an inch; still, it takes me a while to adjust to the smaller proportion. I wanted to share this with you because I know you'll experience the same brief sense of disappointment. The good news is that once the borders are added, the landscape looks imposing again.

The first rule to keep in mind when selecting a border for a landscape is THERE ARE NO RULES! Each quilt has a unique personality and care must be taken to choose a border that will enhance but not overpower. My thoughts about borders have expanded since I wrote the first Impressionist Landscape book. I used to recommend a one-inch inner border, but now I prefer to cut the border a little wider or a little narrower, and I generally choose a tone-on-tone print rather than a solid color. Occasionally I make the inner border a few inches wider than the outer border. This gives a mat and frame effect. (You can find an example of this treatment on page 52.) Lately I've been making landscapes that don't require borders at all. In fact, adding a border would upset the balance of color. Instead of bordering the vase quilts and *Lily Pond Bridge II* (page 118), I had them framed. I also framed the quilt shown on the opposite page. When you make quilts the size of paintings, framing is a nice option to have, and a lovely way to display them.

Here are some general guidelines for selecting borders:

Try not to purchase border fabrics until after the landscape is sewn. That way you can keep an open mind about the colors.

Choose the outer border first. It should be a simple tone-on-tone print; nothing with too much personality because you don't want it to compete with your landscape.

When you take your quilt top to the fabric store, interview several different colors for the outer border…one of them is bound to give the landscape a nice glow. You will need one yard.

After choosing the outer border, you can select a suitable inner border. It could be a contrasting color or the same color as the outer border, but in a lighter value. Study the quilts in this book for ideas. You will need a quarter yard.

You can give your landscape a little more pizzazz by adding a narrow middle border. Refer to the example on page 25. You will need an eighth yard.

A mitered corner treatment is preferable because it gives the illusion of a frame, so make sure when you start cutting strips to cut them the full length of the quilt plus double the width of the finished border (plus an extra two or three inches for good measure). The following border widths are optional and can be changed to suit the dictates of an individual quilt.

Cut four 2"-wide strips (or four 1"-wide strips, whichever you prefer) for the inner border. Cut four ⅞" strips for the optional middle border. Cut four 4" strips for the outer border.

Using a ¼" seam allowance, sew the four inner border strips to the middle border strips (if you choose to use them) and then add the four outer border strips. Press all the seam allowances toward the outer border. Sew a border strip to each side of the landscape, leaving ¼" unsewn at each corner. Miter the four corners. If you don't know how to make mitered corners, consult one of many basic sewing books you probably already own, or check the recommended reading list on page 126.

QUILTING

Quilting stitches are like frosting on a cake. They enhance the appearance and make the texture ever so much better! I enjoy quilting by hand. It's soothing, almost like meditation, and when I quilt in the evening, it gives me an excuse to watch a sitcom without feeling guilty. Machine quilting is nice, too, and there are some advantages: It's fast, and when it's done expertly, it's an art form unto itself.

The quilting design I've chosen for these Impressionist Landscapes is an overall diagonal grid. When viewed from a distance, the stitching pattern catches the light and encourages the illusion of a painting. The borders are quilted with parallel lines to give the impression of a beveled frame. Of course there are many possible ways to quilt these landscapes and you may come up with a solution that expresses your creativity in a different but equally effective manner.

Baste your landscape and batting to a good quality 100% cotton fabric backing. I prefer a radial basting technique because I think it is more appropriate for lap quilting.

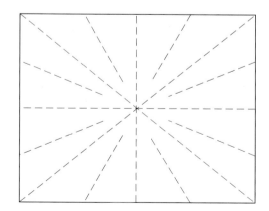

Radial Basting Pattern

Quilt your landscape by hand or machine, using your own pattern or the one suggested in the quilting diagram.

For hand quilting: The finished landscape should look smooth and flat. Mountain Mist® Quilt Light®, Fairfield Low-Loft®, and Fairfield Soft Touch® are excellent batting choices.

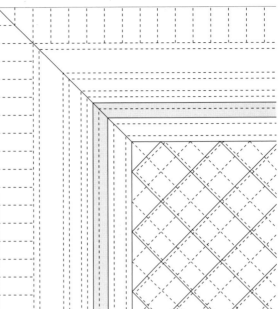

Since the quilting pattern is designed to give an overall texture without being obvious, it is advisable to change the color of your quilting thread to match the different areas. A medium shade of green thread seems to work the best in all the flower areas. Use your favorite brand of quilting thread.

Quilting Diagram (Shaded area is the optional middle border.)

For machine quilting: Choose the thin cotton batting of your choice and a clear filament thread for quilting the landscape area. Use a matching color thread for the borders.

Blocking the landscape: When quilting is complete, set the landscape on your ironing board. Adjust the iron for a medium-warm, synthetic setting.

Carefully press the front of the quilt using a gentle flow of steam. This procedure is like blocking a sweater; it gives the quilt a beautifully finished look.

Do not use a hot iron or your synthetic batting will melt!

BINDING

The binding fabric should be the same as the outer border. Measure the length and width of the quilt and then cut four 2" strips to the appropriate length. Fold the strips in half and press. Using a 1/4" seam allowance, machine stitch the raw edge of the strips to the front of the quilt. Fold over and hand stitch to the back.

Lily Pond Bridge II, 1996, 36" x 41½", Gai Perry

THOUGHTS ON CREATIVITY

Lately, I've been thinking a lot about creativity. Is it something a person is born with? Can it be developed? My dictionary defines it as an "artistic or intellectual inventiveness." I think creativity is learning to see the obvious in a less obvious way. Whatever it is, I know it can't be turned on and off like a light switch. Some days, when I'm designing quilts, I feel as though my hands are touched by magic…other days nothing goes right. I used to worry about these dry spells. I tried working through them but the results were usually uninspired. Now I've learned to shift my creative gears and do something else. For instance, yesterday I started wallpapering our entrance hall. Today I wrote the last section of this book. Tomorrow I might wake up with an idea for a new quilt and spend the next several days totally immersed in its development. If you can give yourself permission to be flexible, life can be one delightfully creative experience after another.

Learn to see the creative alternatives. By the time a two-day Impressionist Landscape class is through, my students tell me they'll never look at fabric the same way again. For example, I've used this lovely wisteria fabric in several landscapes. Wisteria grows naturally in a downward direction, but one of my inventive students turned the square upside down and used the fabric to plant a patch of wild lupine under her version of *The Incredible Flowering Tree*.

These vertically growing hollyhocks can look like a meadow of wildflowers simply by changing the angle of the square.

Alter the direction of this sparkling water fabric to give the impression of distant foliage.

QUESTIONS AND ANSWERS

Here are answers to the questions I'm most frequently asked about the Impressionist Landscapes.

Question: Where do you get your ideas and inspiration?

Answer: Mostly from art books and magazines. The public library is a rich source of information. Sometimes a new floral fabric will inspire me, or every once in a while I manage to take a decent photo of a scene that has struck an emotional cord. Frequently, I'll just start arranging a few squares on my design wall and hope for divine inspiration.

Question: You've made so many Impressionist Landscape quilts, where do you find the time?

Answer: When people ask me this question, I know they don't realize quilting is my profession. I don't keep strict office hours but some days I'll start working at five in the morning and when my husband comes home and asks, "What's for dinner honey?," I can't believe the day is over. I feel blessed to be getting paid for doing something that is so much fun.

Question: How do you know when a landscape is finished?

Answer: I rely on experience, intuition, and my reducing glass. When I look through the glass I want to see all the different areas and elements blending together in perfect color harmony. I don't want to notice individual squares or an area that overpowers the rest of the composition. Most importantly, I want to get an emotional response from the landscape and I want to be moved by the beautiful colors and contrasts.

Question: How can I become more creative?

Answer: I suggest that you make an effort to "think obtuse." Bad grammar but a good idea. When I have a design problem to solve, I try to think around it. I put the problem in the center of an imaginary circle and let all the probable and improbable solutions revolve around it. With this unorthodox approach, I may just come up with an original and workable idea.

Question: How do you store your fabric?

Answer: I've always stored my fabric by color but when I started collecting landscape fabrics, it made more sense to store them by element. I put all the grass textures in one pile, the water textures in another, and so on. I subdivide the flowers into print-scale categories: meadow flowers, individual flowers for 2¼" squares, and larger flowers. The advantage to sorting fabric this way—with all the colors mixed together—is that it widens the opportunity to discover unusual combinations and blends.

Question: How do you store your quilts?

Answer: These landscapes are heavily quilted and tend to crease easily. My solution was to buy six-foot lengths of three-inch diameter PVC pipe at a hardware store. I wash the pipes thoroughly and cover them with bleached muslin (using a glue stick to secure the muslin). Then I can roll as many as six quilts on each cylinder and store them upright in a closet.

Question: Have you ever thought of making an Impressionist Landscape quilt to put on a bed?

Answer: No. I think of these landscapes as pictures. They're designed on a vertical surface and should be viewed on a wall. The compositions are perfectly suited to the size of large paintings.

Question: Do you ever get tired of making Impressionist Landscapes?

Answer: Occasionally I do, but I'm always lured back by an irresistible new piece of fabric or a brilliant landscape made by one of my students. (Teaching can be a two-way street. Sometimes I feel like I'm learning just as much from my students as they're learning from me. It's a nice symbiosis.)

Question: Do you have a favorite Impressionist Landscape quilt?

Answer: Yes, but it's always changing. Usually it's the one I've just finished making.

❧❧❧

One final thought on creativity and the Impressionist Landscape series: In the introduction I said that both quilts and women have come a long way in three-hundred years, but I think there's still a little more traveling to do. Every once in a while I attend one of my husband's business functions and during the course of the evening someone (usually a man) will ask me what I do to keep busy. I enthusiastically reply that I make quilts. I can see his eyes glaze over as he tries to think of something appropriate to say. Invariably he replies, "My grandmother made quilts," and I politely answer, "How nice." End of conversation.

In spite of an occasional lack of sensitivity, quilting has evolved from a basic necessity to a multi-million dollar industry. It's now a recognized art form, and quilts can be found on the walls of museums and corporations. Quilters can browse the Internet, or go into an on-line "chat" room to exchange information and ideas. We can design patterns on our computers and print them in color. Even sewing machines have become computerized. What's next, I can't even imagine!

Postscript

The whole time I was writing this section, I kept thinking about the wisteria fabric and fields of wild lupine. I forced myself to finish these last few pages and the moment I was through, I started cutting out squares. The result is the quilt shown below. As I said…just one delightfully creative experience after another!

Wild Lupine, 1996, 53½" x 37", Gai Perry

TEMPLATE PATTERNS

Photocopy permission on page 2.

    All the template patterns are based on multiples of the 1¾" finished square. With this assortment, you will have the flexibility to cut just about any size flower (or group of flowers). The rectangular shapes are perfect for flowers such as tulips and iris. Try replacing some of the squares in the design with rectangles to add variety to the quilt. *Note:* ¼" seam allowances are already added to all the template patterns.

7½" (7" FINISHED)

5¾" (5¼" FINISHED)

4" (3½" FINISHED)

2¼" (1¾" FINISHED)

1⅜"
(⅞" FINISHED)

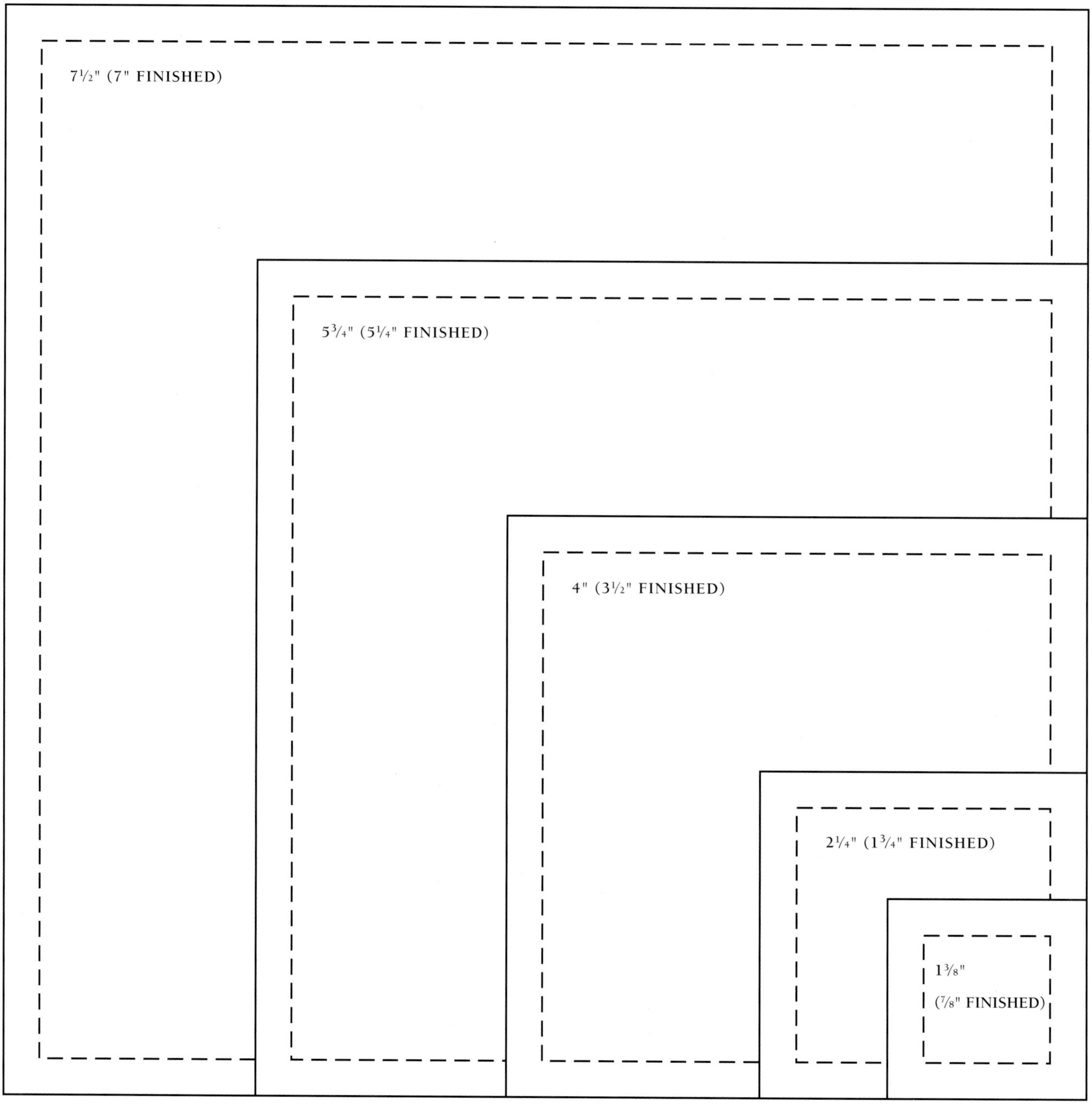

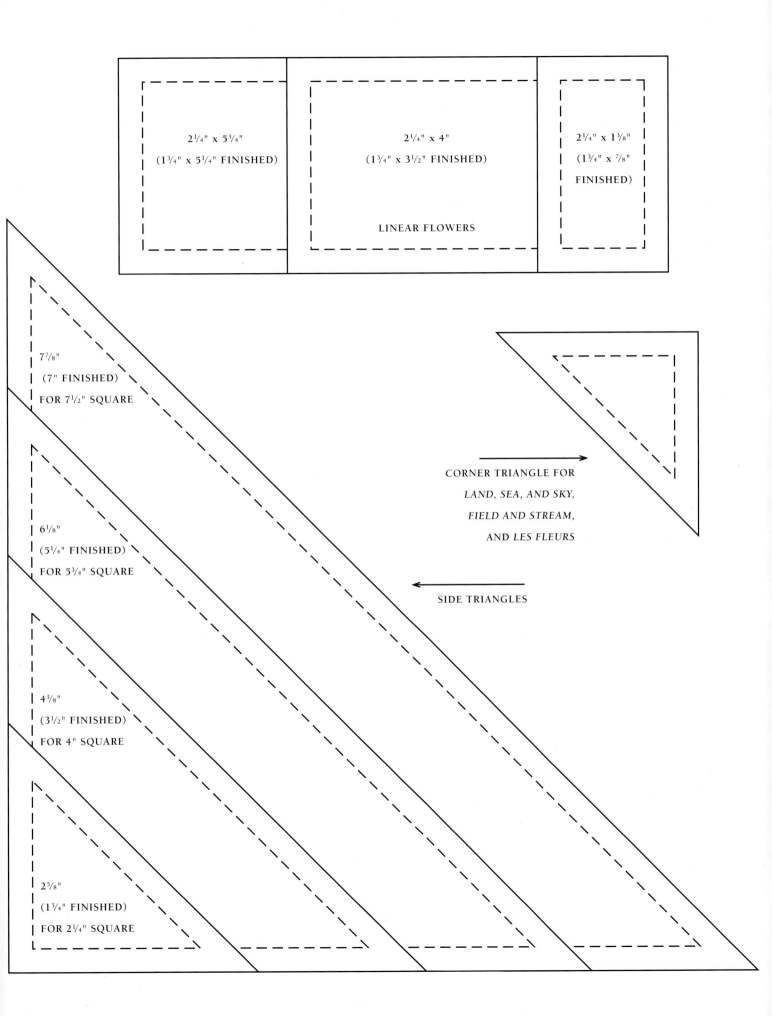

2¼" x 5¾"
(1¾" x 5¼" FINISHED)

2¼" x 4"
(1¾" x 3½" FINISHED)

2¼" x 1⅜"
(1¾" x ⅞"
FINISHED)

LINEAR FLOWERS

CORNER TRIANGLE FOR
LAND, SEA, AND SKY,
FIELD AND STREAM,
AND LES FLEURS

SIDE TRIANGLES

7⅞"
(7" FINISHED)
FOR 7½" SQUARE

6⅛"
(5¼" FINISHED)
FOR 5¾" SQUARE

4⅜"
(3½" FINISHED)
FOR 4" SQUARE

2⅝"
(1¾" FINISHED)
FOR 2¼" SQUARE

BIBLIOGRAPHY

Birren, Faber. *Color in Your World*
New York: MacMillian Publishing Co., Inc., 1962

Birren, Faber. *Creative Color*
West Chester, PA: Schiffer Publishing Ltd., 1987

Itten, Johannes. *The Elements of Color*
New York: The Vendome Press, 1995

Perry, Gai. *Impressionist Quilts*
Lafayette, CA: C&T Publishing, 1995

Basic Quilting Techniques

McClun, Diana and Nownes, Laura. *Quilts! Quilts!! Quilts!!! The Complete Guide to Quiltmaking*
San Francisco: The Quilt Digest Press, 1988

McClun, Diana and Nownes, Laura. *Quilts, Quilts, and More Quilts!*
Lafayette, CA: C&T Publishing, 1993

Art and Gardening Books with Inspirational Photographs

Fell, Derek. *The Impressionist Garden*
New York: Carol Southern Books, 1994

Gerdts, William H. *Monet's Giverny, An Impressionist Colony*
New York: Abbeville Press, 1993

Griffel, Lois. *Painting the Impressionist Landscape*
New York: Watson-Guptill Publications, 1994

House, John. *Monet, Nature into Art*
New Haven: Yale University Press, 1984

Murray, Elizabeth. *Monet's Passion*
San Francisco: Pomegranate Artbooks, 1989

Trenton, Patricia and Gerdts, William H. *California Light 1900-1930*
San Francisco: Bedford Art Publishers, 1990

ABOUT THE AUTHOR

Gai Perry was introduced to quiltmaking in 1981 and fell head-over-heals in love with this uniquely American craft. She has been a full-time quilter ever since.

In 1985, Gai started teaching quilting at local shops and quilt seminars through-out California and Oregon. Because of her fondness for early American antiques, her focus was on the effective use of color and fabric in traditional-style quilts.

By 1990, Gai had a desire to start painting again, but instead of working with paint and brushes, she developed an origi-nal quilting style she named "The Art of the Impressionist Landscape." Her first book, *Impressionist Quilts*, was so well received that she was encouraged to write a follow-up book, and *Impressionist Palette* is the result.

Gai lives with her husband in Walnut Creek, California.

Other Fine Books From C&T Publishing:

Appliqué 12 Easy Ways! Elly Sienkiewicz
Art & Inspirations: Ruth B. McDowell, Ruth B. McDowell
Art & Inspirations: Judith Baker Montano
The Art of Silk Ribbon Embroidery, Judith Baker Montano
The Artful Ribbon, Candace Kling
Baltimore Album Quilts, Historic Notes and Antique Patterns, Elly Sienkiewicz
Baltimore Beauties and Beyond (2 Volumes), Elly Sienkiewicz
Colors Changing Hue, Yvonne Porcella
Crazy with Cotton, Diana Leone
Dimensional Appliqué: Baskets, Blooms & Baltimore Borders, Elly Sienkiewicz
Everything Flowers: Quilts from the Garden, Jean and Valori Wells
The Fabric Makes the Quilt, Roberta Horton
Faces & Places: Images in Appliqué, Charlotte Warr Andersen
Fractured Landscape Quilts, Katie Pasquini Masopust
From Fiber to Fabric: The Essential Guide to Quiltmaking Textiles, Harriet Hargrave
Impressionist Quilts, Gai Perry
Imagery on Fabric (Second Edition), Jean Ray Laury
Landscapes & Illusions, Joen Wolfrom
On the Surface: Thread Embellishment & Fabric Manipulation, Wendy Hill
The Magical Effects of Color, Joen Wolfrom
Patchwork Persuasion: Fascinating Quilts from Traditional Designs, Joen Wolfrom
Quilts for Fabric Lovers, Alex Anderson

Quilts from the Civi;l War, Quilts, Quilts, and More Quilts! Diana McClun and Laura Nownes
Say It with Quilts, Diana McClun and Laura Nownes
Six Color World, Yvonne Porcella
Start Quilting with Alex Anderson: Six Projects for First-Time Quilters, Alex Anderson
Symmetry: A Design System for Quiltmakers, Ruth B. McDowell
The Visual Dance: Creating Spectacular Quilts, Joen Wolfrom

For quiltmaking supplies, call or write to:

Cotton Patch Mail Order
1456 Hall Lane, Dept. CTB
Lafayette, CA 94549
e-mail: cottonpa@aol.com
(800) 835-4418
(510) 283-7883

For more information write for a free catalog from:

C&T Publishing, Inc.
P.O. Box 1456
Lafayette, CA 94549
(800) 284-1114
http://www.ctpub.com

INDEX

borders
    creating 115
    mitered corners 116

color
    blue 23
    colorway 105
    enrichment 30, 38
    fall colors 28
    families 31
    green 22
    influence 25
    orange 23
    questionnaire 17, 39
    red 22
    schemes 32–37
    spectrum 21
    spring colors 26
    subjective palette 9, 17, 41
    summer colors 27
    theory 17
    twelve-color circle 18
    violet 24
    vocabulary 14–15, 18–20
    winter color 29
    yellow 24
color schemes
    analogous 36
    complementary 35
    harmonious 32
    monochromatic 33
    neutral 34
    polychromatic 37
colorway 105
construction method 110–113
contrast
    fabric scale 38
    personality 38
    saturation 38
    value 38
    warm-cool colors 11, 38

design board
    making 62–63
    supplies 62
diagonal grid 62–63, 70
element prints
    cutting 61
    foliage 55
    grass 54
    hill 57
    leaf 54
    mountain 57
    object 58
    path 58

    sky 57
    water 56

fabric
    collecting 43
    cutting flowers 59, 60
    cutting strips 61
    cutting triangles 60
    element prints 53–58, 61
    floral prints 44–51
    flower scale 46
    individual flowers 46
    reverse side 43, 49
    selecting 43
    solids 44, 68
    storing 121
    wonder prints 44, 45, 73, 99
flowers
    arranging 76
    collage 105
    combining 45, 50
    cutting 59–61
    far-distance 49
    flower-leaf transition 48
    for 2 1/4" squares 46
    for 4" squares 46–47
    grow in masses 48
    inappropriate 51
    mid-distance 49

Impressionist Landscape
    creativity 119, 121
    color schemes 32–37
    inspiration 120
    painting 67
    patch appliqué 69
    process 64–65
    projects 71, 72, 78, 86, 92, 98, 104
    selecting fabrics 31, 43
    sewing 9, 101, 107, 109–113
    technique 7, 31, 37, 38, 39, 43, 45, 53, 64, 67, 115
    vocabulary 14–15
    workshop 43
Impressionist Quilts 8, 17, 87, 127

master diagram 65, 71, 74, 80, 88, 94, 100, 106
master diagram, alternate 96, 103

patterns, template 124-125

quilts
    After the Storm 97

April Showers, May Flowers 26
Asilomar: Monterey County 77
Broken Dishes 32
California Winterscape 29
Fall Collage 28
Field and Stream 92
Fifth Season 66
Fourth of July and Berry Pie 27
Full Spectrum Garden, detail 21
Hydrangeas 37
Imagine This 84
In the Garden 91
In the Pink 85
Juin 85
Land, Sea, and Sky 72
Les Fleurs 104
Lily Pond Bridge II 1, 118
Monet's Garden IV 86
Moorea Bay 77
Pieceful Valley 97
Poppy Fields 10
Reflections 52, 53
Serendipity 91
Serenity Bay 6
The Flower Bed 30
The Incredible Flowering Tree 78
The Window Box 42
Vase with White Roses 4
Victorian Bouquet 98
Whispers in Lavender 91
Wild Lupine 123
Woodland Tulips 25

quilting
    binding 117
    blocking 117
    hand 117
    radial basting 116
    machine 117
    overview 116

quiltmakers
    Adrian, Cheron 84
    Cavanaugh, Katherine 91, 97
    Creason, Pamela 85
    Howlett, Judy 77
    Keeton, Barbara 85, 91
    May, Terése 91
    Perry, Gai 1, 4, 6, 10, 21, 26, 27, 28, 29, 30, 32, 42, 66, 72, 78, 86, 92, 104, 118, 123
    Shewey, Billie 97
    Stringer, Pamela 77

subjective palette 9, 17, 41